# SPECTRUM® MATH

## Grade 4

On select pages, you will see a QR code for an instructional video that corresponds to the skills. Videos are also available on carsondellosa.com and YouTube @CarsonDellosaPublishingGroup.

Not sure how to use a QR code?

- Open your smartphone's built-in camera app
- Point the camera at the QR code
- Tap the link that appears on your screen

**CREDITS**
Editor: Jennifer B. Stith
Cover Design: J.J. Giddings, Nick Pearson, Lynne Schwaner
Interior Design: Lynne Schwaner
Illustrations: Lynne Schwaner

Spectrum®
An imprint of Carson Dellosa Education
PO Box 35665
Greensboro, NC 27425  USA

© 2024 Carson Dellosa Education. Except as permitted under the United States Copyright Act, no part of this publication may be reproduced, stored, or distributed in any form or by any means (mechanically, electronically, recording, etc.) without the prior written consent of Carson Dellosa Education. Spectrum® is an imprint of Carson Dellosa Education.

Printed in the USA • All rights reserved.
ISBN 978-1-4838-7147-9
01-1062412735

# Table of Contents Grade 4

**Spectrum Introduction** ........................... 4
**Chapter 1:** Adding and Subtracting ............. 6
Pretest Chapter 1 .................................. 8
Lesson 1.1 Adding 1- and 2-Digit Numbers ....... 10
Lesson 1.2 Subtracting 1- and 2-Digit
    Numbers ...................................... 11
Lesson 1.3 Adding Three or More 1-Digit
    Numbers ...................................... 12
Lesson 1.4 Adding 2-Digit Numbers with
    Regrouping .................................... 13
Lesson 1.5 Adding Three or More 2-Digit
    Numbers ...................................... 14
Lesson 1.6 Subtracting 2 Digits from 3 Digits with
    Regrouping .................................... 16
Lesson 1.7 Thinking Subtraction for Addition ..... 18
Lesson 1.8 Thinking Addition for Subtraction ..... 19
Lesson 1.9 Using Compatible Numbers to
    Subtract ....................................... 20
Lesson 1.10 Problem Solving ..................... 21
Posttest Chapter 1 ................................ 22
**Chapter 2:** Place Value .......................... 24
Pretest Chapter 2 ................................. 26
Lesson 2.1 Understanding Place Value to
    Hundreds ..................................... 28
Lesson 2.2 Understanding Place Value to
    Hundred Thousands ........................... 29
Lesson 2.3 Rounding ............................. 30
Lesson 2.4 Comparing Numbers .................. 32
Posttest Chapter 2 ................................ 34
**Chapter 3:** Adding and Subtracting 3-, 4-, and
    5-Digit Numbers .............................. 36
Pretest Chapter 3 ................................. 38
Lesson 3.1 Adding 3-Digit Numbers .............. 40
Lesson 3.2 Subtracting 3-Digit Numbers ......... 41
Lesson 3.3 Adding 4-Digit Numbers .............. 42
Lesson 3.4 Problem Solving ...................... 43
Lesson 3.5 Subtracting 4- and 5-Digit
    Numbers ...................................... 44
Lesson 3.6 Adding Three or More Numbers
    (through 4 digits) ............................. 46

Lesson 3.7 Adding 4- and 5-Digit
    Numbers ...................................... 47
Lesson 3.8 Problem Solving ...................... 48
Lesson 3.9 Addition and Subtraction
    Practice ....................................... 49
Lesson 3.10 Problem Solving ..................... 51
Posttest Chapter 3 ................................ 52
**Chapter 4:** Multiplication ....................... 54
Pretest Chapter 4 ................................. 56
Lesson 4.1 Prime and Composite Numbers ....... 58
Lesson 4.2 Interpreting Equations ................ 60
Lesson 4.3 Multiplying 2-Digit by 1-Digit
    Numbers ...................................... 61
Lesson 4.4 Multiplying 2-Digit by 1-Digit Numbers
    with Regrouping .............................. 62
Lesson 4.5 Problem Solving ...................... 63
Lesson 4.6 Multiplying 3-Digit by 1-Digit Numbers
    with Regrouping .............................. 64
Lesson 4.7 Multiplying 2-Digit by 2-Digit Numbers
    with Regrouping .............................. 65
Lesson 4.8 Multiplying 3-Digit by 2-Digit Numbers
    with Regrouping .............................. 67
Lesson 4.9 Multiplying 4-Digit by 1-Digit Numbers
    with Regrouping .............................. 68
Lesson 4.10 Problem Solving ..................... 69
Posttest Chapter 4 ................................ 70
**Chapter 5:** Division ............................. 72
Pretest Chapter 5 ................................. 74
Lesson 5.1 Dividing Multiples of 10 and 100 ..... 76
Lesson 5.2 Dividing through 45 ÷ 5 .............. 77
Lesson 5.3 Dividing through 63 ÷ 7 .............. 78
Lesson 5.4 Dividing through 81 ÷ 9 .............. 79
Lesson 5.5 Division Practice ..................... 80
Lesson 5.6 Problem Solving ...................... 81
Lesson 5.7 Dividing 2-Digits by 1-Digit .......... 82
Lesson 5.8 Dividing 3-Digits by 1-Digit .......... 84
Lesson 5.9 Dividing 4-Digits by 1-Digit .......... 86
Lesson 5.10 Problem Solving ..................... 88
Posttest Chapter 5 ................................ 90
**Learning Checkpoint** Chapters 1–5 ............ 92
**Chapter 6:** Fractions ............................ 98

# Table of Contents Grade 4

Pretest Chapter 6............................100
Lesson 6.1 Finding Equivalent Fractions..........102
Lesson 6.2 Comparing Fractions Using
    Models...................................103
Lesson 6.3 Comparing Fractions Using the
    LCM......................................104
Lesson 6.4 Adding Fractions with Like
    Denominators..........................105
Lesson 6.5 Subtracting Fractions with Like
    Denominators..........................106
Lesson 6.6 Decomposing Fractions...........107
Lesson 6.7 Problem Solving....................108
Lesson 6.8 Understanding Decimals to
    Tenths...................................109
Lesson 6.9 Understanding Decimals to
    Hundredths............................110
Lesson 6.10 Adding Fractions with Unlike
    Denominators..........................111
Lesson 6.11 Adding Mixed Numbers with
    Like Denominators....................112
Lesson 6.12 Subtracting Mixed Numbers
    with Like Denominators.............113
Lesson 6.13 Problem Solving...................114
Lesson 6.14 Fractions as Multiples..............115
Lesson 6.15 Multiplying Fractions and Whole
    Numbers.................................116
Lesson 6.16 Problem Solving...................117
Posttest Chapter 6............................118
**Chapter 7**: Measurement.....................120
Pretest Chapter 7............................122
Lesson 7.1 Customary Units of Length..........126
Lesson 7.2 Problem Solving....................127
Lesson 7.3 Customary Units of Capacity........128
Lesson 7.4 Customary Units of Weight..........129
Lesson 7.5 Problem Solving....................130
Lesson 7.6 Metric Units of Length..............131
Lesson 7.7 Metric Units of Capacity............132
Lesson 7.8 Metric Units of Weight..............133
Lesson 7.9 Problem Solving....................134
Lesson 7.10 Measuring Perimeter...............135
Lesson 7.11 Measuring Area....................136

Lesson 7.12 Problem Solving....................137
Lesson 7.13 Line Plots in Measurement..........138
Lesson 7.14 Identifying Angles..................139
Lesson 7.15 Measuring and Drawing Angles......140
Lesson 7.16 Finding Missing Angles..............141
Posttest Chapter 7............................142
**Chapter 8**: Geometry.........................146
Pretest Chapter 8............................148
Lesson 8.1 Points, Rays, and Angles............149
Lesson 8.2 Parallel, Intersecting, and
    Perpendicular Lines....................150
Lesson 8.3 Symmetrical Shapes.................152
Lesson 8.4 Quadrilaterals.......................154
Lesson 8.5 Triangles............................155
Posttest Chapter 8............................156
**Chapter 9**: Preparing for Algebra.............158
Pretest Chapter 9............................160
Lesson 9.1 Extending Patterns with Addition......162
Lesson 9.2 Extending Patterns with Subtraction...163
Lesson 9.3 Extending Patterns with Multiplication.164
Lesson 9.4 Extending Patterns with Division......165
Lesson 9.5 Growing Number Patterns with
    Changing Rules........................166
Lesson 9.6 Problem Solving....................167
Posttest Chapter 9............................168
**Learning Checkpoint** Chapters 6–9............170
**Final Test** Chapters 1–9......................175
**Scoring Record for Chapter Posttests, Learning
Checkpoints, and Final Test**....................183
**Answer Key**..................................184

Spectrum Math Grade 4

# Spectrum Introduction

For more than 20 years, Spectrum® workbooks have been the solution for helping students meet and exceed learning goals. Each title in the Spectrum workbook series offers grade-appropriate instruction and reinforcement in an effective sequence for learning success.

Spectrum partners with you in supporting your student's educational journey every step of the way! This book will help them navigate Grade 4 math and will give you the support you need to make sure they learn everything they need to know. Inside you will find:

# Chapter Introductions

These introductions provide useful information about the chapter. They may include:

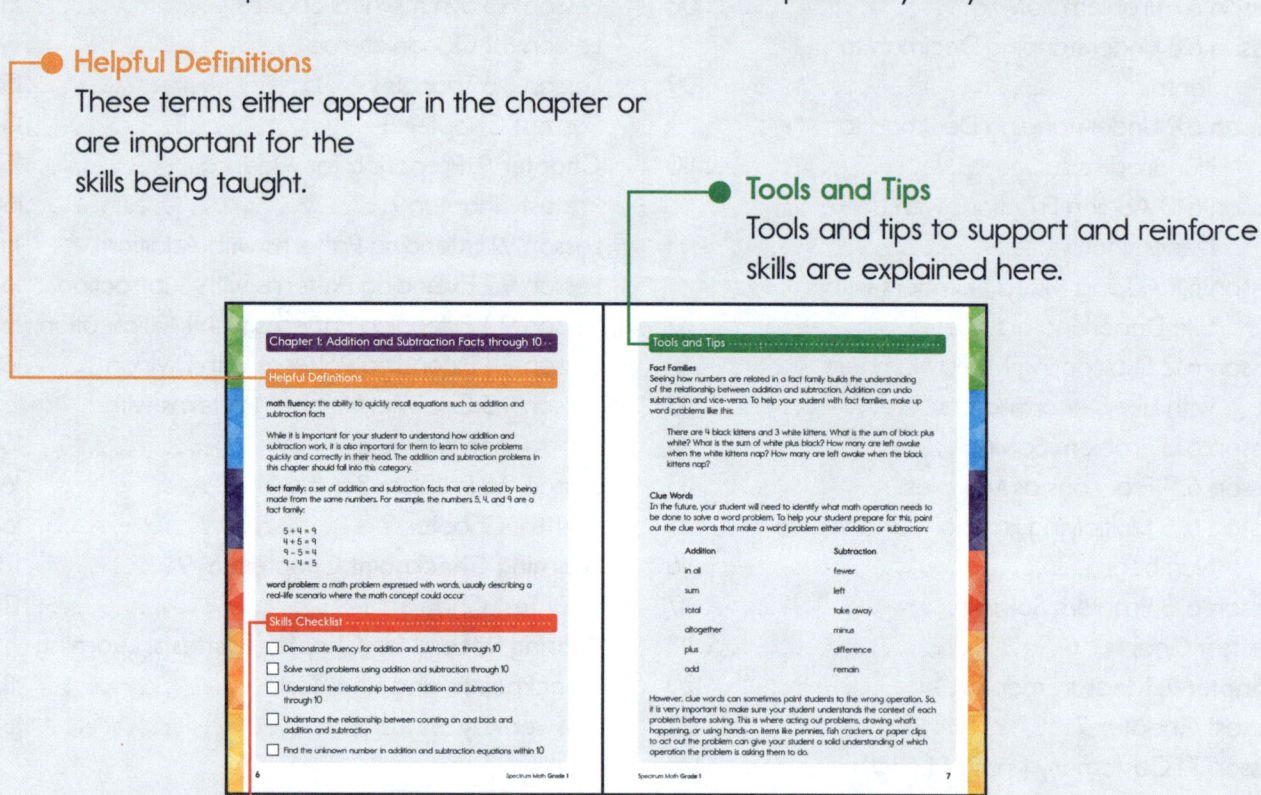

### Helpful Definitions
These terms either appear in the chapter or are important for the skills being taught.

### Tools and Tips
Tools and tips to support and reinforce skills are explained here.

### Skills Checklist
This checklist helps ensure your student is practicing grade-level skills.

Spectrum Math Grade 4

## Lessons

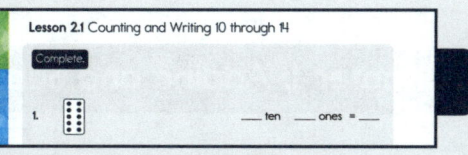

These pages begin with a definition, step-by-step instructions where needed, and examples, followed by independent practice.

## Enrichment

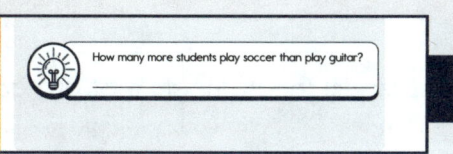

These problems appear throughout the book. They allow your student to dig deeper and apply the skill they learned in a different way than it is practiced on the page. The two types of problems will ask your student to think critically and explain reasoning.

## Pretests

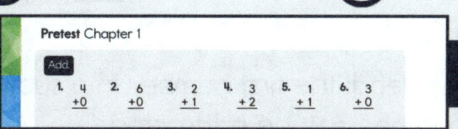

These quick skill assessments serve as a starting point for the chapter. They will include the skills covered in the chapter and allow your student to gage what they already know and what they need extra practice with.

## Posttests

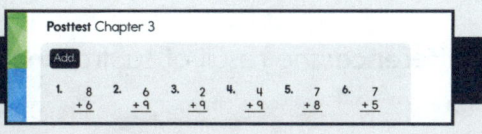

These end-of-chapter assessments test to see if your student gained the skills they needed from the chapter they just completed. You can compare these tests to the pretests and measure your student's growth.

## Learning Checkpoints

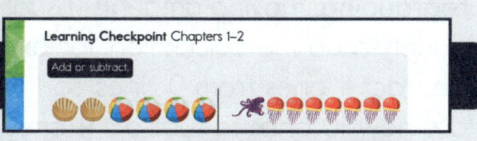

These reviews break up the book into halfway points to prepare your student for the final test.

## Final Test

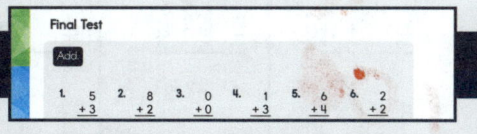

This test covers the skills learned in the book. Use this comprehensive test to assess what your student has learned and to identify what they still need to work on.

## Answer Key

The answers to the lessons, reviews, and tests are provided in an answer key.

Spectrum Math Grade 4

# Chapter 1: Adding and Subtracting

## Helpful Definitions

**addends:** the numbers that are added together

**sum:** the result of adding two or more numbers

$$\begin{array}{r} \text{addend} \longrightarrow \phantom{+}3 \\ \text{addend} \longrightarrow +4 \\ \hline \text{sum} \longrightarrow \phantom{+}7 \end{array}$$

**minuend:** the first number in a subtraction problem; the number from which another number is to be subtracted

**subtrahend:** the second number in a subtraction problem; the number that is to be subtracted

**difference:** the result of subtracting one number from another

$$\begin{array}{r} \text{minuend} \longrightarrow \phantom{-}10 \\ \text{subtrahend} \longrightarrow -\phantom{0}4 \\ \hline \text{difference} \longrightarrow \phantom{-0}6 \end{array}$$

**regrouping:** moving amounts (usually 10) from one part of a calculation to another so it is easier to do the calculation; for example, in the problem below, it is not possible to subtract 4 ones from 0 ones, so 1 ten needs to be regrouped into 10 more ones. There are now 10 ones to subtract 4 ones from.

$$\begin{array}{r} 120 \\ -14 \\ \hline \end{array} \quad \begin{array}{r} \phantom{1}10 \\ 12\cancel{0} \\ -14 \\ \hline \end{array} \quad \begin{array}{r} \phantom{1}10 \\ 12\cancel{0} \\ -14 \\ \hline 6 \end{array} \quad \begin{array}{r} \phantom{1}10 \\ 12\cancel{0} \\ -14 \\ \hline 06 \end{array} \quad \begin{array}{r} \phantom{1}10 \\ 12\cancel{0} \\ -14 \\ \hline 106 \end{array}$$

Spectrum Math Grade 4

## Skills Checklist

- [ ] Adding and subtracting multi-digit numbers
- [ ] Using regrouping strategies when subtracting
- [ ] Using subtraction to check addition answers
- [ ] Using addition to check subtraction answers
- [ ] Solving real-world problems with addition and subtraction

## Tools and Tips

To develop a solid understanding of basic addition and subtraction facts, this chapter focuses heavily on addition and subtraction. Fact fluency is essential for algebraic concepts learned in fifth and sixth grade.

When your student sees a problem such as 25 + 11, they use what they know about basic facts and decomposing tens and ones to add. Add the ones. Then, add the tens.

$$25 + 11 = 20 + 5 + 10 + 1$$
$$30 + 6 = 36$$
$$25 + 11 = 36$$

In the problem 26 − 13, they can decompose the problem into tens and ones. Subtract the ones. Then, subtract the tens.

$$26 - 13 = 20 + 6 - 10 + 3$$
$$10 + 3 = 13$$
$$26 - 13 = 13$$

Your student will also see problems that require them to regroup numbers, such as 61 − 12. Because you cannot subtract a large number from a smaller number, your student needs to know to regroup 1 ten into 10 ones. Then, they can subtract the ones and tens.

$$61 - 12 = \overset{50}{\cancel{60}} + \overset{11}{\cancel{1}} - 10 + 2$$
$$40 + 9 = 49$$
$$61 - 12 = 49$$

Spectrum Math Grade 4

Name _____

**Pretest** Chapter 1

Add or subtract.

1.  12
   + 7

2.  35
   + 3

3.  55
   +23

4.  42
   + 7

5.  32
   +25

6.  13
   +12

7.  56
   +13

8.  43
   +24

9.  54
   +33

10. 54
    +23

11. 36
    +12

12. 75
    +24

13. 25
    −12

14. 49
    −27

15. 57
    −46

16. 75
    −23

17. 29
    −15

18. 89
    −27

19. 45
    − 4

20. 59
    −48

21. 54
    −42

22. 79
    −27

23. 27
    − 6

24. 65
    −55

Name _____

## Pretest Chapter 1

**Solve each problem.**  **Show your work.**

**25.** There are 42 pages in Sasha's comic book. Last night, Sasha read 18 pages. How many more pages does she have left to read?

There are _____ pages left to read.

**26.** Mr. Mehta has 13 new students in his fourth-grade class. He already has 22 students in the class. How many students are in Mr. Mehta's class?

There are _____ students in his class.

**27.** Wei and Nadia want to throw a surprise party for Omar. They plan to send 35 invitations. If Wei writes 23, how many invitations does Nadia need to write?

Nadia needs to write _____ invitations.

**28.** Mateo's lacrosse team is in the playoffs. There were 22 goals made in the first game. Mateo's team made 13 of them. How many goals were scored by the other team?

The other team scored _____ goals.

Spectrum Math Grade 4

9

Name _____

## Lesson 1.1 Adding 1- and 2-Digit Numbers

When adding multi-digit numbers, add the ones first. Then, add the tens.

```
  2 3        2 3        2 3
+ 1 6      + 1 6      + 1 6
              9        3 9
```

**Add.**

1.  11
   + 8

2.  10
   + 3

3.  25
   + 4

4.  81
   + 8

5.  52
   + 7

6.  74
   +23

7.  20
   +30

8.  41
   + 8

9.  50
   +11

10. 20
   +15

11. 46
   +21

12. 34
   +34

13. 60
   +13

14. 35
   +12

15. 51
   +48

How does knowing 4 + 5 = 9 help you solve 40 + 50? Explain.

_____

_____

10

Spectrum Math Grade 4

Name _____

# Lesson 1.2 Subtracting 1- and 2-Digit Numbers

When subtracting multi-digit numbers, subtract the ones first. Then, subtract the tens.

```
  5 3          5 3          5 3
- 2 1        - 2 1        - 2 1
               ___          ___
                 2          3 2
```

**Subtract.**

| | | | |
|---|---|---|---|
| 1.    3 3<br>− 1 2 | 2.    4 3<br>− 2 0 | 3.    9 1<br>− 3 0 | 4.    7 6<br>− 1 1 |
| 5.    2 7<br>− 1 0 | 6.    1 8<br>− 1 3 | 7.    3 8<br>− 2 7 | 8.    9 7<br>− 3 3 |
| 9.    4 9<br>− 8 | 10.    9 4<br>− 1 3 | 11.    8 7<br>− 5 | 12.    7 1<br>− 2 0 |
| 13.    8 5<br>− 6 3 | 14.    1 5<br>− 1 1 | 15.    9 9<br>− 7 | 16.    6 2<br>− 1 2 |

Spectrum Math Grade 4

Name _____

## Lesson 1.3 Adding Three or More 1-Digit Numbers

When adding more than two addends, look for facts you know such as doubles facts or making 10 facts.

```
  3
  5 } 6
+ 3
        6
      + 5
      ——
       11

  2
  7 } 10
+ 3
        10
      +  2
      ——
       12

  3
  4
  1 } 5
+ 2
        5
      + 5
      ——
       10
```

**Add.**

| 1. | 3 | 2. | 2 | 3. | 7 | 4. | 6 | 5. | 8 |
|---|---|---|---|---|---|---|---|---|---|
|   | 4 |   | 6 |   | 5 |   | 3 |   | 7 |
|   | +5 |   | +3 |   | +3 |   | +7 |   | +2 |

| 6. | 9 | 7. | 3 | 8. | 1 | 9. | 4 | 10. | 3 |
|---|---|---|---|---|---|---|---|---|---|
|   | 9 |   | 6 |   | 7 |   | 6 |   | 5 |
|   | +1 |   | +8 |   | +6 |   | +8 |   | +2 |

| 11. | 1 | 12. | 2 | 13. | 2 | 14. | 5 | 15. | 1 |
|---|---|---|---|---|---|---|---|---|---|
|   | 7 |   | 8 |   | 2 |   | 5 |   | 7 |
|   | 5 |   | 3 |   | 7 |   | 4 |   | 6 |
|   | +1 |   | +6 |   | +1 |   | +3 |   | +4 |

Spectrum Math Grade 4

Name _____

## Lesson 1.4 Adding 2-Digit Numbers with Regrouping

If the digits in the ones column add to more than 9, regroup the ten to the tens column.

```
     45          ¹             ¹
   + 36         45            45
                +36           +36
                  1            81

            Add the ones.  Add the tens.
            5 + 6 = 11     1 + 4 + 3 = 8
```

**Add.**

1.  27      2.  78      3.  27      4.  55
   +38         +13         +47         +26

5.  29      6.  19      7.  56      8.  27
   +18         +15         +19         +45

9.  37     10.  48     11.  52     12.  77
   +26         +14         +28         +15

13. 47     14.  65     15.  75     16.  39
   +33         +25         +18         +17

Spectrum Math Grade 4

Name _____

## Lesson 1.5 Adding Three or More 2-Digit Numbers

```
   26        2           2
   38       26          26
  +56       38          38
           +56         +56
            ─           ───
            0          120
```
Add the ones.    Add the tens.
6 + 8 + 6 = 20    2 + 2 + 3 + 5 = 12

**Add.**

1.  27
    32
   +43

2.  39
    48
   +76

3.  48
    68
   +78

4.  97
    85
   +63

5.  45
    74
   +48

6.  97
    23
   +19

7.  77
    99
   +32

8.  38
    57
   +75

9.  92
    89
   +95

10. 37
    29
   +49

11. 87
    78
   +95

12. 38
    49
   +57

14

Spectrum Math Grade 4

Name _____

## Lesson 1.5 Adding Three or More 2-Digit Numbers

**Add.**

1.  37
    26
    +43

2.  59
    40
    +16

3.  27
    88
    +53

4.  42
    24
    +38

5.  97
    23
    +19

6.  81
    19
    +38

7.  38
    57
    +75

8.  19
    37
    +49

9.  66
    57
    73
    +35

10. 27
    53
    68
    +74

11. 22
    17
    39
    +45

12. 57
    33
    71
    +66

13. 19
    38
    42
    +76

14. 39
    49
    46
    +32

15. 21
    62
    54
    +38

16. 35
    37
    49
    +91

Write one strategy you use to add three or more addends.

_____

_____

Spectrum Math Grade 4

15

# Lesson 1.6 Subtracting 2 Digits from 3 Digits with Regrouping

$$\begin{array}{r} {}^{4}1\cancel{5}\cancel{3}^{13} \\ -\phantom{0}37 \\ \hline 6 \end{array}$$

Subtract the ones.
(Regroup 5 tens to 4 tens and 10 ones. Rename 3 ones as 13 ones.)

$$\begin{array}{r} {}^{4}1\cancel{5}\cancel{3}^{13} \\ -\phantom{0}37 \\ \hline 16 \end{array}$$

Subtract the tens.

$$\begin{array}{r} {}^{4}1\cancel{5}\cancel{3}^{13} \\ -037 \\ \hline 116 \end{array}$$

Subtract the hundreds.

**Subtract.**

1. 175 − 38
2. 132 − 17
3. 175 − 66
4. 134 − 29

5. 156 − 38
6. 182 − 73
7. 177 − 59
8. 123 − 18

9. 141 − 33
10. 173 − 54
11. 141 − 29
12. 193 − 47

13. 152 − 37
14. 172 − 29
15. 154 − 68
16. 145 − 26

# Lesson 1.6 Subtracting 2 Digits from 3 Digits with Regrouping

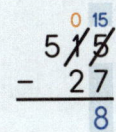

$$\begin{array}{r} \phantom{0}^{0}5^{15}\!\!\!\!\!\!\!\phantom{5}1\phantom{5} \\ -\phantom{0}27 \\ \hline 8 \end{array}$$

Subtract the ones.
(Regroup 1 ten to 0 tens and 10 ones. Rename 5 ones as 15 ones.)

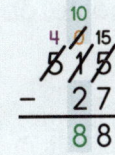

$$\begin{array}{r} ^{4}\!5^{10}\!1^{15} \\ -\phantom{0}27 \\ \hline 88 \end{array}$$

Subtract the tens.
(Regroup the 5 hundreds to 4 hundreds and 10 tens. Rename 0 tens as 10 tens.)

$$\begin{array}{r} ^{4}\!5^{10}\!1^{15} \\ -027 \\ \hline 488 \end{array}$$

Subtract the hundreds.

**Subtract.**

1.  275
    − 97

2.  182
    − 94

3.  366
    − 89

4.  127
    − 58

5.  134
    − 42

6.  361
    − 94

7.  125
    − 38

8.  281
    − 95

9.  442
    − 84

10. 153
    − 67

11. 525
    − 83

12. 275
    − 94

Explain why, in the problems above, it is important to subtract the ones and then subtract the tens.

_____

_____

Spectrum Math Grade 4

17

Name _____

## Lesson 1.7 Thinking Subtraction for Addition

Addition and subtraction are inverse, or opposite, operations. Use one to check your answer for the other.

```
   55
 + 43
 ----
   98
 - 43
 ----
   55
```

To check if 55 + 43 = 98, subtract 43 from 98.

These numbers should be the same.

**Add. Then, check your answer.**

1.  32      2.  63      3.  38      4.  28
   +47         +19         +24         +15
   ___         ___         ___         ___

   ___         ___         ___         ___

5.  75      6.  28      7.  39      8.  48
   +15         +27         +32         +27
   ___         ___         ___         ___

   ___         ___         ___         ___

9.  199     10. 128     11. 109     12. 137
   + 14        + 33        + 32        + 29
   ___         ___         ___         ___

   ___         ___         ___         ___

18

Spectrum Math Grade 4

Name _____

## Lesson 1.8 Thinking Addition for Subtraction

Subtraction and addition are inverse, or opposite, operations. Use one to check your answer for the other.

```
   1 3 8
 -   2 4
   1 1 4
 +   2 4
   1 3 8
```

To check 138 − 24 = 114, add 24 to 114.

These numbers should be the same.

**Subtract. Then, check your answer.**

1.   98
    −44

    + ___

2.   24
    −18

    + ___

3.   57
    −38

    + ___

4.   84
    −26

    + ___

5.   97
    −63

    + ___

6.   28
    −17

    + ___

7.   67
    −26

    + ___

8.   53
    −36

    + ___

9.   142
    − 63

    + ___

10.  179
    − 82

    + ___

11.  137
    − 52

    + ___

12.  155
    − 28

    + ___

Spectrum Math Grade 4

19

Name _____

## Lesson 1.9 Using Compatible Numbers to Subtract

Another way to subtract two numbers is to make one number easier to work with.

Let's solve 64 − 17.

```
  64 + 3 =   67
− 17 + 3 = − 20
            47
```

Avoid regrouping by making one of the numbers a multiple of ten. Add 3 to 17 to make 20. You must also add 3 to the 64. Now, subtract easily.

Let's solve 300 − 74.

```
  300 − 1 =   299
−  75 − 1 = −  74
              225
```

Avoid regrouping by subtracting 1 from 300. It is easier to subtract from 9s.

**Use compatible numbers to subtract.**

1.  79
   −15

2.  92
   −87

3.  49
   −37

4.  82
   −54

5.  202
   − 75

6.  149
   − 92

7.  400
   −188

8.  601
   − 26

9.  348
   − 13

20

Spectrum Math Grade 4

Name _____

## Lesson 1.10 Problem Solving

**Solve each problem.**  **Show your work.**

1. Anthony Adams needs to sell 195 candy bars to raise money for the school robotics club. He already sold 109 bars. How many more candy bars does he have to sell?

   He has to sell _____ more candy bars.

2. Bookmarks had a book drive for a local school. On Monday, the store collected 85 books. They collected 81 more books on Tuesday. How many books did the store collect?

   Bookmarks collected _____ books.

3. The Garcia family went on a camping trip. Their cabin is 235 miles away. If they drive 98 miles the first day, how many more miles do they have to drive to get to the cabin?

   They must drive _____ more miles.

4. The community center had an all-you-can-eat pizza party for all elementary school students. They bought 215 slices of cheese pizza and 120 slices of pepperoni pizza. How many slices of pizza did they buy?

   They bought _____ slices of pizza.

Spectrum Math Grade 4

Name _____

## Posttest Chapter 1

**Add or subtract.**

1.  38
   +15

2.  73
   +27

3.  46
   +21

4.  137
   + 28

5.  238
   + 68

6.  156
   + 48

7.  103
   + 18

8.  432
   + 48

9.  73
    21
   +10

10. 14
    18
   +12

11. 105
    92
   + 14

12. 81
    68
   +43

13. 98
   −25

14. 88
   −16

15. 81
   −63

16. 105
   − 16

17. 215
   − 26

18. 192
   − 48

19. 173
   − 28

20. 402
   − 79

Name _____

**Posttest** Chapter 1

Solve each problem.　　　　　　　　　　　　　　　　　　Show your work.

21. Ms. Freese and her students are collecting cans to recycle. The girls have 55 cans, the boys have 32 cans, and Ms. Freese has 13 cans. How many cans do they have altogether?

    They collected _____ cans.

22. The dance team is raising money by running a car wash. They need to wash 110 cars to raise enough money. They have washed 78 cars already. How many more cars do they need to wash?

    They need to wash _____ more cars.

23. Mr. Brown's science class is studying the environment around the school. Students observed 37 different plants and 15 different animals. How many plants and animals did the class observe altogether?

    The class found _____ plants and animals.

24. Shay and Reese found frog eggs in a pond. Shay found 92 eggs and Reese found 108 eggs. How many frog eggs did they find?

    They found _____ frog eggs.

Spectrum Math Grade 4

## Chapter 2: Place Value

### Helpful Definitions

**place value**: the value of a digit determined by its position in a number
Writing a number in a place value chart can help your student determine the value of each digit.

| Hundred Thousands | Ten Thousands | Thousands | Hundreds | Tens | Ones |
|---|---|---|---|---|---|

729,865

**rounding**: a way to replace a number with a number that is close in value and easier to work with; look at the digit to the right of the place you are rounding to; for example:
    Round 2,746 to the nearest thousand.
    2,746
    Look at the place to the right of the thousands place. The digit 7 is more than 5, so 2,746 rounds up to 3,000 when rounded to the nearest thousand.

    Round 53,429 to the nearest ten thousand.
    Look at the place to the right of the ten thousands place. The digit 3 is less than 5, so 53,429 rounds down to 50,000 when rounded to the nearest ten thousand.

**expanded form**: a way of writing numbers according to the place value of each digit
    346 = 300 + 40 + 6
    792,105 = 700,000 + 90,000 + 2,000 + 100 + 5

**inequalities**: statements in which the numbers are not equal; for example:
These symbols are used to compare numbers. The symbols < and > show inequalities.
    345 > 125    345 is greater than 125.
    233 < 678    233 is less than 678.

## Skills Checklist

☐ Reading and writing numbers using numerals, expanded form, and words

☐ Rounding numbers to the nearest ten thousand, hundred thousand, and million

☐ Comparing numbers using symbols > (greater than), < (less than), and = (equal to)

## Tools and Tips

**Place Value Helpers**
Numbers are all around us! We find them on price tags for the toy your student wants to buy and in stats for their favorite sports player. Your student will use place value knowledge to read, write, and understand numbers like these.

When your student sees a digit, such as 5, they need to be able to determine the value of it. Is the value 5, 50, or 500? The value of the digit is determined by where it is found in the number. In the number 354, for example, the 5 is in the tens place. Since there are 5 tens, the value of the 5 is 50. However, in the number 35, the 5 is in the ones place. The value of 5 ones is 5.

Use a stack of 6 disposable foam cups that have a rim. Turn each cup on its side and write the digits 0–9 vertically along the rim on each cup. Have your student start with three cups and nest them. Turn the cups to practice making 3-digit numbers. Encourage your student to add more cups and make greater numbers.

**Run and Round!**
To reinforce rounding numbers, use a life-size number line! With sidewalk chalk, draw a number line from 0 to 9 to show the one-digit numbers that could appear in any place of a number. Then, draw a line dividing the number line in half (between the 4 and the 5). Explain that if a digit is found in the first half of the number line, run toward the zero to round down. If the digit is found in the second half of the number line, run toward the 9 to round up. Practice giving your student different numbers and asking them to run to the end of the number line to show if they should round down or up.

Spectrum Math Grade 4

Name _____

**Pretest** Chapter 2

Write each number in expanded form.

1. 51 _____

2. 973 _____

3. 2,675 _____

4. 1,265 _____

5. 84,740 _____

6. 790,036 _____

Write each number in word form.

7. 945 _____

8. 4,337 _____

9. 52,082 _____

10. 628,400 _____

11. 496,529 _____
_____

12. 367,414 _____
_____

26

Spectrum Math Grade 4

Name _____

# Pretest Chapter 2

**Compare each pair of numbers. Write >, <, or =.**

13. 3,214 ◯ 3,412        14. 95 ◯ 92          15. 408 ◯ 480

16. 56,250 ◯ 56,520      17. 572 ◯ 570        18. 150,009 ◯ 15,009

19. 8,416 ◯ 8,461        20. 43,116 ◯ 34,116  21. 8,910,070 ◯ 8,910,070

**Round each number to the place indicated.**

22. hundreds   932 _____

23. thousands   7,649 _____

24. tens   1,675 _____

25. ten thousands   82,397 _____

26. hundreds   732,005 _____

27. hundred thousands   553,972 _____

**Write the value of the 1 in each number.**

28. 15,235 _____    29. 419 _____

30. 8,176,235 _____  31. 509,321 _____

32. 794,167 _____    33. 910,308 _____

Spectrum Math Grade 4

27

Name _____

# Lesson 2.1 Understanding Place Value to Hundreds

Each digit in a number has a value based on its position in the number.

The place and value of the 2 in each number is different.

    12    2 ones, or 2
    23    2 tens, or 20
   208   2 hundreds, or 200

Expanded form is an expression that shows each digit's value as an addition problem.

    54    50 + 4
   673   600 + 70 + 3
   105   100 + 5

**Write each number in expanded form.**

1. 430 _____
2. 549 _____
3. 549 _____
4. 608 _____
5. 201 _____
6. 907 _____
7. 554 _____
8. 312 _____

**Write the number or word form.**

9. one hundred thirty-two _____
10. five hundred thirteen _____
11. eighty-seven _____

12. 852 _____
13. 119 _____
14. 595 _____

**Write the value of the digit in each place named.**

15. tens: 872 _____
16. hundreds: 934 _____
17. ones: 663 _____
18. tens: 795 _____

28

Spectrum Math Grade 4

Name _____

# Lesson 2.2 Understanding Place Value to Hundred Thousands

**Write each number in expanded form.**

1. 653,410 _____

2. 76,982 _____

3. 103,234 _____

4. 199,482 _____

5. 32,451 _____

6. 8,430 _____

**Write the word form for each number.**

7. 85,034 _____

8. 11,987 _____

9. 153,721 _____

10. 968,425 _____

**Write the digit in each place named.**

11. ten thousands: 50,975 _____

12. hundred thousands: 986,580 _____

13. thousands: 79,802 _____

14. ten thousands: 546,671 _____

15. ten thousands: 865,003 _____

16. hundred thousands: 297,780 _____

Explain how the expanded forms of 2,007 and 2,397 are different.

_____

_____

Spectrum Math Grade 4

29

# Lesson 2.3 Rounding

**Rounding** numbers means simplifying a number but keeping its value close to the original number. To round to a specific place, look at the digit to the right of that place. If the digit on the right is 0–4, the left digit stays the same. If the digit on the right is 5–9, the left digit goes up.

Round 274 to the nearest ten.

2 7 4
↓
2 7 0

Round 278 to the nearest ten.

2 7 8
↓
2 8 0

**Round to the nearest ten.**

1. 6,421
2. 5,882
3. 45,288
4. 975

**Round to the nearest hundred.**

5. 67,523
6. 4,378
7. 8,564
8. 79,342

**Round to the nearest thousand.**

9. 74,150
10. 2,933
11. 62,465
12. 9,731

Name _____

# Lesson 2.3 Rounding

Round 284,830 to the nearest ten thousand.

2 8 4 , 8 3 0   Look at the thousands digit. 4 is less than five, so 8 stays the same.
↓
2 8 0 , 0 0 0   Follow with zeros.

**Round to the nearest ten thousand.**

1. 184,564 _____

2. 735,567 _____

3. 34,596 _____

4. 638,744 _____

**Round to the nearest hundred thousand.**

5. 745,129 _____

6. 157,241 _____

7. 435,900 _____

8. 576,132 _____

Explain how you know if you round up or down.

_____

Spectrum Math Grade 4

Name _____

# Lesson 2.4 Comparing Numbers

To **compare numbers**, look at each place in the numbers from left to right. Use comparison symbols > (greater than), < (less than), or = (equal to).

Compare 35 and 42.

   3 5    4 2    Look at the tens place in each number.
(3 0 < 4 0)    30 is less than 40.
   3 5 < 4 2    So, 35 is less than 42.

Compare 117 and 114.

   1 1 7   1 1 4    Look at the hundreds place in each number. They are the same.
   1 1 7   1 1 4    Look at the tens place in each number. They are the same.
   1 1 7   1 1 4    Look at the ones place in each number.
     (7 > 4)    7 is greater than 4.
   1 1 7 > 1 1 4    So, 117 is greater than 114.

Compare 59 and 59.

   5 9    5 9    Look at the tens. They are the same.
   5 9    5 9    Look at the ones. They are the same.
   5 9 = 5 9    So, 59 is equal to 59.

**Compare each pair of numbers. Write >, <, or =.**

1. 105 ◯ 120      2. 52 ◯ 35      3. 1,036 ◯ 1,056

4. 5,002 ◯ 2,005      5. 713 ◯ 731      6. 2,317 ◯ 1,713

7. 1,170 ◯ 1,070      8. 232 ◯ 323      9. 142 ◯ 142

10. 616 ◯ 106      11. 919 ◯ 920      12. 1,036 ◯ 1,056

Name _____

# Lesson 2.4 Comparing Numbers

**Write numbers to complete the expressions. The lines indicate how many digits long each number should be.**

1. __ __ < __ __

2. __ __ = __ __

3. __ __ > __ __

4. __ __ __ > __ __ __

5. __ __ __ < __ __ __

6. __ __ __ > __ __ __

7. __,__ __ __ = __,__ __ __

8. __,__ __ __ > __,__ __ __

9. __ __,__ __ __ < __ __,__ __ __

10. __ __,__ __ __ < __ __,__ __ __

**Compare each pair of numbers with >, <, or =.**

11. 71,023 ◯ 71,320

12. 9,789 ◯ 9,780

13. 6,896 ◯ 6,886

14. 506,708 ◯ 506,807

15. 49,984 ◯ 49,984

16. 600,080 ◯ 608,000

Can you write a comparison of two different numbers whose digits are 2, 4, 6, and 8? Try it!

_____

Spectrum Math Grade 4

33

Name _____

**Posttest** Chapter 2

Write each number in expanded form.

1. 965,012 _____

2. 693,145 _____

3. 103,458 _____

4. 23,972 _____

5. 471,440 _____

6. 18,321 _____

Write the word form for each numeral.

7. 5,012 _____

8. 102 _____

9. 1,141 _____

10. 99,612 _____

11. 834,763 _____

12. 21,817 _____

Name _____

## Posttest Chapter 2

**Round each number to the nearest thousand.**

13. 5,012 _____    14. 7,801 _____

15. 1,141 _____    16. 98,612 _____

17. 834,763 _____    18. 21,817 _____

**Round each number to the nearest hundred thousand.**

19. 651,298 _____    20. 198,205 _____

21. 519,190 _____    22. 457,213 _____

23. 509,815 _____    24. 385,921 _____

**Compare each pair of numbers. Write >, <, or =.**

25. 24,124 ◯ 24,224          26. 975,212 ◯ 985,212

27. 56,410 ◯ 54,408          28. 609,712 ◯ 690,172

29. 724,100 ◯ 724,101        30. 2,019 ◯ 2,109

Spectrum Math Grade 4

35

# Chapter 3: Adding and Subtracting 3-, 4-, and 5-Digit Numbers

## Helpful Definitions

**place value:** the value of a digit determined by its position in a number

A place value chart can be used to keep digits properly aligned when adding or subtracting. Remind your student that they should always start on the right and move to the left in the place value chart when adding or subtracting numbers.

| Hundreds | Tens | Ones |
|---|---|---|
| 3 | 6 | 7 |
| − 1 | 3 | 4 |
| 2 | 3 | 3 |

| Ten Thousands | Thousands | Hundreds | Tens | Ones |
|---|---|---|---|---|
| 1 | 5 | 3 | 8 | 9 |
| + | 1 , | 3 | 1 | 0 |
| 1 | 6 , | 6 | 9 | 9 |

**regrouping:** the process of making groups of ten in order to add or subtract numbers

| Subtract the ones. | Subtract the tens. First, regroup 1 hundred into 10 tens. | Subtract the hundreds and thousands. |
|---|---|---|
| 2,422<br>− 1,391<br>1 | 3 12<br>2,4̸2̸2<br>− 1,391<br>31 | 3 12<br>2,4̸2̸2<br>− 1,391<br>1,031 |

3 12
2,4̸2̸2
− 1,391
1,031

The hundred cube is regrouped into 10 tens rods.

36

Spectrum Math Grade 4

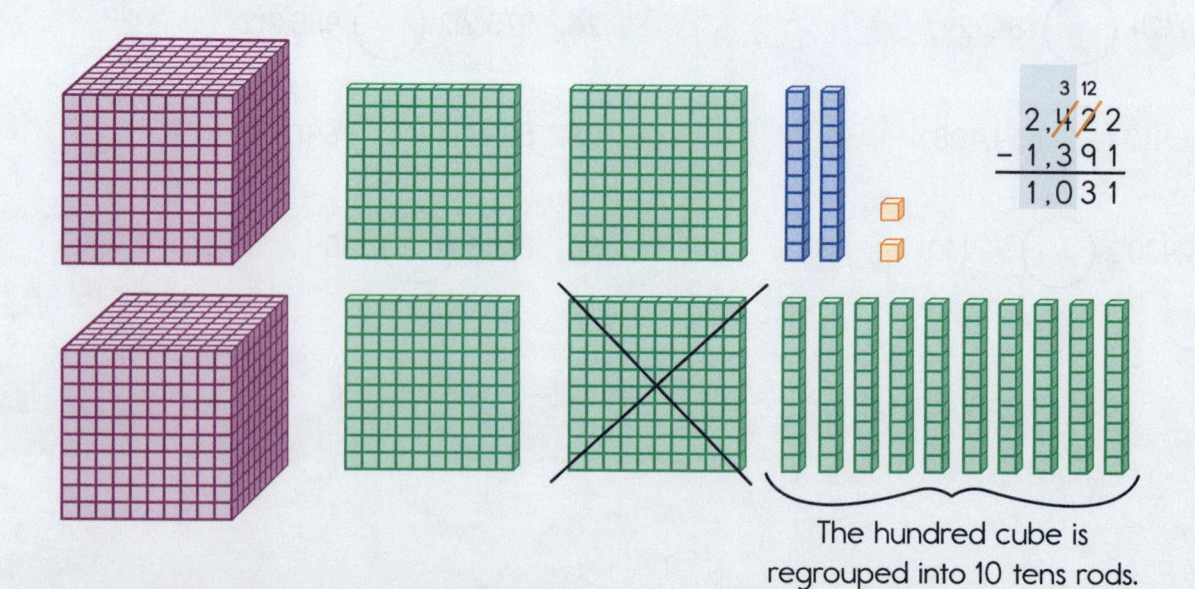

## Skills Checklist

☐ Adding and subtracting numbers up to 5 digits, regrouping as needed

☐ Using addition and subtraction to solve real-world problems

☐ Adding 3 or more numbers

## Tools and Tips

Adding and subtracting are frequently used skills in daily life. Your student has likely mastered addition and subtraction facts. Now they will continue to add and subtract greater numbers with up to 5 digits. These numbers represent real-life situations, such as the number of tickets the fourth-grade class sold for a school raffle or the total number of students at your student's school.

You and your student will see and use numbers in your daily lives. Point out chances to use numbers and have your student add or subtract them. For example, when driving on a family trip, point out the total number of miles you will travel and the number of miles you have traveled so far. Have your student subtract the numbers to determine how many more miles you have left to go.

Name _____

**Pretest** Chapter 3

**Add.**

1. 562
 + 217

2. 1,452
 +  519

3. 732
 + 195

4. 5,606
 + 1,324

5. 4,003
 + 1,717

6. 1,930
 +  117

7. 2,281
 + 1,307

8. 1,502
 +  375

9. 3,007
 + 2,993

10. 6,423
 +  314

11. 3,489
 + 1,301

12. 2,811
 + 1,187

**Subtract.**

13. 867
 − 314

14. 987
 − 445

15. 760
 − 352

16. 757
 − 152

17. 2,872
 −  591

18. 1,890
 −  727

19. 5,799
 −  418

20. 8,648
 −  526

21. 4,103
 −  136

22. 2,378
 − 1,060

23. 9,057
 − 3,152

24. 3,817
 − 1,404

Name _____

**Pretest** Chapter 3

Solve each problem.

Show your work.

25. The Haven Humane Society took in 3,875 pets in the first six months of the year. The rest of the year, they took in 1,455 pets. How many pets did they take in during the year?

    They took in _____ pets during the year.

26. Springfield School District bought 1,570 new science books. There are 1,976 students in the science classes. How many students will not receive a new book?

    There will be _____ students without a new book.

27. Erik had to ride a bus for 1,472 miles to get to Ashland City. The bus broke down after 1,227 miles. How many more miles did Erik have to travel?

    He had _____ miles left to travel.

28. Taryn is getting ready to go to basketball camp. There are 213 players arriving on Friday and 131 players arriving on Saturday. If 104 players arrive on Sunday including Taryn, then how many total players will be at the camp?

    There will be _____ players at the camp.

Spectrum Math Grade 4

39

# Lesson 3.1 Adding 3-Digit Numbers

```
   356          356         ¹356         ¹356
 +253        +253         +253         +253
              ───          ───          ───
                9           09          609
```

                  Add the ones.    Add the tens.    Add the hundreds.
                                    Regroup 10 tens into
                                        1 hundred.

**Add.**

| | a | | b | | c | | d |
|---|---|---|---|---|---|---|---|
| 1. | 727<br>+182 | 2. | 503<br>+247 | 3. | 482<br>+107 | 4. | 132<br>+127 |
| 5. | 663<br>+125 | 6. | 823<br>+170 | 7. | 337<br>+224 | 8. | 281<br>+224 |
| 9. | 407<br>+313 | 10. | 804<br>+179 | 11. | 503<br>+307 | 12. | 723<br>+177 |
| 13. | 448<br>+136 | 14. | 294<br>+103 | 15. | 956<br>+142 | 16. | 243<br>+109 |

Spectrum Math Grade 4

# Lesson 3.2 Subtracting 3-Digit Numbers

```
  1,748            1,748            1,7⁶¹⁴8           ⁰₁⁶,⁶7¹⁴8
-   952          -   952          -    952          -    952
                        6               96               796
```

                Subtract the ones.    Regroup and     Regroup and subtract
                                    subtract the tens.     the hundreds.

**Subtract.**

1.     992
      − 367

2.     772
      − 621

3.     505
      − 436

4.     887
      − 475

5.    1,763
      −  452

6.    7,036
      −  736

7.    5,521
      −  489

8.    2,440
      −  332

9.    5,280
      −  953

10.   6,578
      −  214

11.   2,159
      −  202

12.   4,236
      −  172

13.   3,882
      −  436

14.   8,146
      −  540

15.   5,374
      −  992

16.   7,325
      −  953

Spectrum Math Grade 4

Name _____

## Lesson 3.3 Adding 4-Digit Numbers

```
  7,564        7,564        7,564        7,564        7,564
+ 4,322      + 4,322      + 4,322      + 4,322      + 4,322
               ─────        ─────        ─────        ─────
                   6           86          886       11,886
```

              Add the ones.    Add the tens.    Add the hundreds.    Add the thousands.

**Add.**

1.    1,576  
  + 1,321

2.    3,309  
  + 1,557

3.    5,094  
  + 2,190

4.    1,887  
  + 1,774

5.    3,113  
  + 2,002

6.    1,720  
  + 2,017

7.    4,025  
  + 1,883

8.    6,754  
  + 1,006

9.    7,430  
  + 2,670

10.    3,552  
  + 4,431

11.    2,882  
  + 1,908

12.    2,473  
  + 1,303

13.    5,005  
  + 2,108

14.    6,754  
  + 3,070

15.    1,847  
  + 1,630

16.    3,070  
  + 2,880

Spectrum Math Grade 4

Name _____

## Lesson 3.4 Problem Solving

**Solve each problem.**   **Show your work.**

1. A moving company moved 3,400 families this year. Last year, the company moved 2,549 families. How many families did the company move in the past two years?

   The company moved _____ families.

2. The pet supply store buys a total of 7,307 crickets every month for lizard food. If the store needs 230 crickets per month to feed their own lizards, how many crickets are left to sell to customers?

   They have _____ crickets left to sell to customers.

3. Neese Nursery sold 561 flowers on Saturday and 359 flowers on Sunday. How many flowers did Neese Nursery sell over the weekend?

   Neese Nursery sold _____ flowers.

4. In one morning, workers packed two crates of soup cans. The first load weighed 1,558 pounds and the second load weighed 1,600 pounds. How many pounds of soup cans did the workers pack that morning?

   The workers packed _____ pounds of cans.

Spectrum Math Grade 4

Name _____

## Lesson 3.5 Subtracting 4- and 5-Digit Numbers

$$\begin{array}{r} 23,546 \\ -\phantom{0}7,643 \\ \hline \end{array}$$

$$\begin{array}{r} 23,546 \\ -\phantom{0}7,643 \\ \hline 3 \end{array}$$ Subtract the ones.

$$\begin{array}{r} 23,546 \\ -\phantom{0}7,643 \\ \hline 03 \end{array}$$ Subtract the tens.

$$\begin{array}{r} {}^{2\phantom{0}15}\phantom{0}\\ 2\cancel{3},\cancel{5}46 \\ -\phantom{0}7,643 \\ \hline 903 \end{array}$$ Regroup and subtract the hundreds.

$$\begin{array}{r} {}^{1\phantom{0}12\phantom{0}15}\\ \cancel{2}\cancel{3},\cancel{5}46 \\ -\phantom{0}7,643 \\ \hline 5,903 \end{array}$$ Regroup and subtract the thousands.

$$\begin{array}{r} {}^{1\phantom{0}12\phantom{0}15}\\ \cancel{2}\cancel{3},\cancel{5}46 \\ -07,643 \\ \hline 15,903 \end{array}$$ Subtract the ten thousands.

**Subtract.**

1. $\begin{array}{r} 26,625 \\ -\phantom{0}6,510 \\ \hline \end{array}$
2. $\begin{array}{r} 73,461 \\ -\phantom{0}3,861 \\ \hline \end{array}$
3. $\begin{array}{r} 40,305 \\ -\phantom{0}6,307 \\ \hline \end{array}$
4. $\begin{array}{r} 66,859 \\ -\phantom{0}4,437 \\ \hline \end{array}$

5. $\begin{array}{r} 85,713 \\ -\phantom{0}7,649 \\ \hline \end{array}$
6. $\begin{array}{r} 30,080 \\ -\phantom{0}2,400 \\ \hline \end{array}$
7. $\begin{array}{r} 87,223 \\ -\phantom{0}5,224 \\ \hline \end{array}$
8. $\begin{array}{r} 95,348 \\ -\phantom{0}6,007 \\ \hline \end{array}$

Name _____

## Lesson 3.5 Subtracting 4- and 5-Digit Numbers

**Subtract.**

1.  80,247
   − 15,136

2.  33,969
   − 20,970

3.  25,845
   − 10,703

4.  57,538
   − 23,888

5.  22,127
   − 15,102

6.  27,791
   − 13,782

7.  67,690
   − 44,085

8.  76,115
   − 24,007

9.  99,818
   − 66,919

10. 39,000
   − 22,002

11. 35,844
   − 24,954

12. 85,784
   − 63,035

13. 36,736
   − 17,621

14. 51,416
   − 27,418

15. 41,764
   − 22,694

16. 98,802
   − 11,070

Can you think of a way to make it easier to complete this operation? Try it!

67,000
− 9,999

Spectrum Math Grade 4

45

Name _____

# Lesson 3.6 Adding Three or More Numbers (through 4 digits)

Add each place value from right to left. Be careful to keep regrouped digits in the correct place value columns.

```
      1              1 1            1 1            1 1
  3,2 5 1        3,2 5 1        3,2 5 1        3,2 5 1
    3 3 5          3 3 5          3 3 5          3 3 5
+   2 4 8      +   2 4 8      +   2 4 8      +   2 4 8
        4             3 4          8 3 4        3,8 3 4
```

Add the ones.     Add the tens.        Add the hundreds.   Add the thousands.
Regroup the ten.  Regroup the hundred.

**Add.**

1.  460        2.  300        3.  605        4.  700
    240            305            245            42
    16             240            113            36
  + 14          + 65          +105          + 29

5.  617        6.  2,012      7.  7,615      8.  1,725
    522            150            1,207          1,528
  +133          + 113         +1,152        +1,341

9.  4,973     10.  3,417     11.  5,009     12.  7,010
    2,007          2,345          4,103          5,528
    1,221          1,132          2,705          3,175
 +1,003         +  305        +1,003        +  948

46                                                     Spectrum Math Grade 4

Name _____

# Lesson 3.7 Adding 4- and 5-Digit Numbers

Add each place value from right to left. Be careful to keep regrouped digits in the correct place value columns.

```
  53,240
+  6,644     Add the ones.
       4
```

```
  53,240
+  6,644     Add the tens.
     884
```

```
  53,240
+  6,644     Add the hundreds.
     884
```

```
  53,240
+  6,644     Add the thousands.
   9,884
```

```
  53,240
+  6,644     Add the ten thousands.
  59,884
```

**Add.**

1. 9,100 + 3,498

2. 5,009 + 5,900

3. 4,880 + 1,744

4. 2,376 + 1,484

5. 23,703 + 6,147

6. 13,778 + 9,093

7. 10,735 + 5,781

8. 45,173 + 3,217

9. 82,048 + 8,953

10. 23,230 + 17,075

11. 32,705 + 18,805

12. 40,119 + 25,118

13. 15,978 + 14,605

14. 14,157 + 13,352

15. 64,576 + 26,640

16. 56,844 + 43,280

Spectrum Math Grade 4

Name _____

## Lesson 3.8 Problem Solving

**Solve each problem.**　　　　　　　　　　　　　　　　　　　　　**Show your work.**

1. Last year, 5,670 students attended Pender Elementary School. This year, 5,732 students are attending the school. How many more students are attending Pender Elementary School this year?

    There are _____ more students attending Pender Elementary School this year.

2. There are about 5,400 species of mammals in the world. There are about 10,000 species of birds. About how many mammals and birds are there in the world?

    There are _____ species of mammals and birds.

3. Over the weekend, the Midway Theater sold 1,208 buckets of popcorn, 2,543 sodas, and 973 boxes of candy. How many concessions did the theater sell?

    The theater sold _____ concessions.

4. At the state fair, the candy booth was very popular. It had a swimming pool filled with chocolate-covered peanuts and pretzels. There was a total of 97,635 pieces of candy in the pool. If the pool contained 56,784 chocolate-covered peanuts, then how many pretzels were there?

    There were _____ pretzels.

Spectrum Math Grade 4

**Name** _____

# Lesson 3.9 Addition and Subtraction Practice

**Add.**

1. 
```
  1,515
+ 1,212
```

2. 
```
  10,763
+  9,276
```

3. 
```
  74,612
+  3,400
```

4. 
```
  9,408
+ 2,592
```

5. 
```
  2,513
    727
+   236
```

6. 
```
   815
   673
+  295
```

7. 
```
  7,035
  3,975
+   713
```

8. 
```
  1,220
    399
+   706
```

**Subtract.**

9. 
```
  5,703
- 2,147
```

10. 
```
  3,814
- 2,616
```

11. 
```
  6,973
- 1,782
```

12. 
```
  7,113
- 6,327
```

13. 
```
  55,013
-  5,907
```

14. 
```
  81,910
-  7,950
```

15. 
```
  49,834
- 26,174
```

16. 
```
  60,704
- 50,913
```

Explain how you know if you will have to regroup digits in an addition problem.

_____

_____

Spectrum Math Grade 4

49

Name _____

# Lesson 3.9 Addition and Subtraction Practice

**Add or subtract.**

1.  6,418
      527
    + 318

2.  1,385
      972
    + 113

3.  5,759
    2,132
    +  784

4.  9,107
    6,048
    +  710

5.   5,117
    − 4,108

6.  1,195
    −  945

7.   7,362
    − 6,119

8.   8,173
    − 7,289

9.   45,009
    + 28,785

10.  12,489
    +  7,981

11.  83,568
    + 49,829

12.  39,975
    + 81,369

13.   8,080
    − 4,092

14.  2,817
    −  250

15.  14,809
    − 12,734

16.  87,672
    − 69,318

17.  92,408
    − 49,802

18.  12,489
    −  5,117

19.  18,873
    − 12,092

20.  79,998
    − 37,948

50

Spectrum Math Grade 4

Name _____

# Lesson 3.10 Problem Solving

**Solve each problem.**

**Show your work.**

1. Roberto and Rene counted the pennies they have been saving for 5 years. Roberto has 52,781 pennies and Rene has 58,972 pennies. How many pennies do they have altogether?

   They have _____ pennies.

2. Mr. Chien's art classes melted down broken crayons to make a wax figure. The morning class melted 7,325 pieces. The afternoon class melted 6,800 pieces. How many pieces did the classes melt?

   The classes melted _____ pieces.

3. There are 5,248 different types of insects in the local forest. Of those, 518 can be harmful to people. How many insects are not harmful?

   _____ insects are not harmful.

4. A baseball team gave away free hats to 10,917 fans. There were 13,786 people at the game. How many fans did not get a free hat?

   _____ fans did not get a free hat.

Spectrum Math Grade 4

51

Name _____

**Posttest** Chapter 3

Add or subtract.

1.    6,280
   +3,770

2.   50,012
   + 1,597

3.    2,118
   −   825

4.    7,381
   −5,964

5.    8,045
   −   210

6.    3,815
   −   356

7.    6,819
   −   910

8.    7,462
   −   720

9.    8,291
      6,104
   +5,596

10.    735
      162
   +  94

11.   2,515
     1,003
   +  714

12.   2,519
     1,943
   +  756

13.  51,372
   − 8,619

14.  39,982
   −17,551

15.  99,895
   −75,872

16.  68,613
   −40,007

52

Spectrum Math Grade 4

Name _____

**Posttest** Chapter 3

Solve each problem.

Show your work.

17. Reva's doctor wants her to walk more for exercise. She has to walk 10,000 steps daily. On Saturday, she only walked 8,972 steps. How many more steps did Reva need to walk?

    She needed to walk _____ more steps.

18. Clay wanted to paint his bedroom either blue or green. At the paint store, there were 785 shades of blue and 685 shades of green. How many color choices did Clay have?

    Clay had _____ color choices.

19. The hospital's service elevator can hold 12,560 pounds. A technician and equipment weigh 752 pounds. How much more weight can the elevator hold?

    The elevator can hold _____ more pounds.

20. Aditi collects stamps from around the world. She has 2,315 stamps so far, but her goal is to have 5,500 stamps. How many more stamps does she need to meet her goal?

    She needs _____ more stamps.

Spectrum Math Grade 4

# Chapter 4: Multiplication

## Helpful Definitions

**factors**: numbers being multiplied to get a product; for example:
**3** × **7** = 21

**composite**: a number that has more than two factors; for example, 9 is a composite number because it has three factors (1, 3, and 9)

1 × 9 = 9

3 × 3 = 9

**prime**: a number that has only the factors 1 and itself; for example, 5 is a prime number because its factors are 1 and 5

1 × 5 = 5

**regrouping**: the process of making groups of ten in order to carry out an operation

```
  1
  2 3
×   6
    8
```
Multiply 3 ones by 6 ones. 3 × 6 = 18
Put the 8 under the ones place. Put the 1 ten above the 2 tens.

```
  1
  2 3
×   6
1 3 8
```
Multiply 2 tens by 6 ones. Then, add 1 ten.
20 × 6 = 120. 120 + 10 = 130

## Skills Checklist

☐ Understanding the difference between prime and composite

☐ Identifying numbers as prime or composite and listing their factors

☐ Writing equations to solve for an unknown number in a word problem

☐ Multiplying multi-digit numbers, regrouping when needed

☐ Solving real-world problems using multiplication

## Tools and Tips

In this chapter, your student will learn to identify the factors of a number. For example, the factors of the number 12 are 1, 2, 3, 4, 6, and 12 (1 × 12 = 12; 2 × 6 = 12; 3 × 4 = 12). Knowing the factors of a number will enable your student to memorize and use basic multiplication facts. Then your student will be able to solve multiplication problems with larger numbers.

Also in this chapter, your student will identify factors of numbers to classify numbers as prime or composite. By breaking down a number into its prime factors, your student will be able to group factors in a way that allows them to solve problems easily.

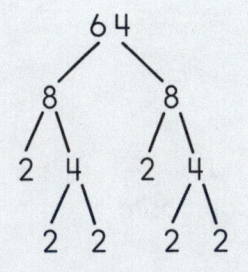

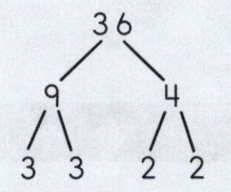

64 = 8 × 8
64 = 4 × 16
64 = 2 × 32

36 = 9 × 4
36 = 6 × 6
36 = 18 × 2

Spectrum Math Grade 4

Name _____

# Pretest Chapter 4

**Multiply.**

1. 7 × 8
2. 25 × 3
3. 302 × 4
4. 17 × 5
5. 10 × 9

6. 12 × 12
7. 315 × 47
8. 29 × 9
9. 91 × 52
10. 32 × 33

11. 403 × 7
12. 193 × 8
13. 605 × 40
14. 3,279 × 21
15. 1,040 × 22

**Write the factors of each number. Then, label it *prime* or *composite*.**

| | Factors | Prime or Composite |
|---|---|---|
| 16. 12 | | |
| 17. 20 | | |
| 18. 11 | | |
| 19. 32 | | |
| 20. 5 | | |

Spectrum Math Grade 4

Name _____

**Pretest** Chapter 4

**Solve each problem.**  **Show your work.**

21. Students set up the chairs for the spring concert at Murray Elementary School. There were 25 rows with 10 chairs in each row. How many chairs did they set up?

    They set up _____ chairs.

22. The town fall carnival was a success. The school sold 99 tickets and each ticket was good for 2 rides. How many rides did the school sell?

    The school sold _____ rides.

23. The cafeteria planned to bake 3 chocolate chip cookies for every student in the school. If there are 715 students, how many cookies does the cafeteria need to bake?

    The cafeteria needs to bake _____ cookies.

24. Chris and Evan have been working 10 hours every week on their presentation. If they work on the presentation for 5 weeks, how many hours will they work on the presentation?

    They will work _____ hours on the presentation.

Spectrum Math Grade 4

Name _____

## Lesson 4.1 Prime and Composite Numbers

A **prime** number's only factors are 1 and itself.
   7 is a prime number; its only factors are 1 and 7.

A **composite** number has more than two factors.
   8 is a composite number; its factors are 1, 2, 4, and 8.

Write the factors of each number. Then, label it *prime* or *composite*.

                    **Factors**                                    *Prime* or *Composite*

1. 64  _____   _____

2. 43  _____   _____

3. 53  _____   _____

4. 72  _____   _____

5. 19  _____   _____

6. 48  _____   _____

7. 22  _____   _____

8. 36  _____   _____

9. 89  _____   _____

10. 31  _____   _____

11. 80  _____   _____

12. 55  _____   _____

Name _____

# Lesson 4.1 Prime and Composite Numbers

**Color each prime number orange. Color each composite number green.**

| 1 | 2 | 3 | 4 | 5 | 6 | 7 | 8 | 9 | 10 |
|---|---|---|---|---|---|---|---|---|---|
| 11 | 12 | 13 | 14 | 15 | 16 | 17 | 18 | 19 | 20 |
| 21 | 22 | 23 | 24 | 25 | 26 | 27 | 28 | 29 | 30 |
| 31 | 32 | 33 | 34 | 35 | 36 | 37 | 38 | 39 | 40 |
| 41 | 42 | 43 | 44 | 45 | 46 | 47 | 48 | 49 | 50 |
| 51 | 52 | 53 | 54 | 55 | 56 | 57 | 58 | 59 | 60 |
| 61 | 62 | 63 | 64 | 65 | 66 | 67 | 68 | 69 | 70 |
| 71 | 72 | 73 | 74 | 75 | 76 | 77 | 78 | 79 | 80 |
| 81 | 82 | 83 | 84 | 85 | 86 | 87 | 88 | 89 | 90 |
| 91 | 92 | 93 | 94 | 95 | 96 | 97 | 98 | 99 | 100 |

True or False: Any number ending in 1 is a prime number. Support your answer with evidence.

_____

_____

Spectrum Math Grade 4

Name _____

## Lesson 4.2 Interpreting Equations

To **interpret an equation**, figure out what information you do know and what you do not know. Use a variable, or letter, to represent that which you do not know.

Reid is 3 years old. His sister Nell is 4 times older. How old is Nell?
Reid is 3.
Nell is 4 × 3. (Her age can be represented by $n$.)
$n = 4 \times 3$
$n = 12$ (Nell is 12 years old.)

**Solve each problem.**   **Show your work.**

1. Tia has 7 hair bows. Her sister Tessa has 6 times as many bows as Tia. How many hair bows does Tessa have?

   Tessa has _____ hair bows.

2. Jay mows 1 lawn every day Monday through Saturday. He is paid $25 for each lawn. How much money does Jay earn each week mowing lawns?

   Jay earns $ _____ each week.

3. Macon eats 33 animal crackers as a snack every day after school. How many animal crackers does he eat during a 5-day school week?

   Macon eats _____ animal crackers.

4. Mari bought 7 packages of greeting cards. Each package had 9 cards. How many greeting cards did she buy in all?

   Mari bought _____ greeting cards.

Name _____

# Lesson 4.3 Multiplying 2-Digit by 1-Digit Numbers

To multiply 2-digit numbers by 1-digit numbers, follow these steps.

```
  3 2     Multiply the ones.        2 × 3 = 6
×   3
    6
```

```
  3 2     Multiply the tens by the ones.    30 × 3 = 90
×   3
  9 6
```

**Multiply.**

1.  23
  ×  2

2.  71
  ×  1

3.  12
  ×  4

4.  33
  ×  2

5.  10
  ×  7

6.  44
  ×  2

7.  43
  ×  2

8.  90
  ×  1

9.  22
  ×  4

10. 12
  ×  3

11. 24
  ×  2

12. 14
  ×  2

13. 11
  ×  9

14. 30
  ×  3

15. 42
  ×  2

16. 11
  ×  7

Spectrum Math Grade 4

61

Name _____

# Lesson 4.4 Multiplying 2-Digit by 1-Digit Numbers with Regrouping

To multiply 2-digit numbers by 1-digit numbers, follow these steps.

$\begin{array}{r}\overset{1}{7}2\\\times\phantom{0}8\\\hline 6\end{array}$   Multiply the ones.  $2 \times 8 = 16$
Put the 6 under the ones and regroup the 1 ten.

$\begin{array}{r}\overset{1}{7}2\\\times\phantom{0}8\\\hline 576\end{array}$   Multiply the tens by the ones.  $70 \times 8 = 560$
Add the extra ten.  $560 + 10 = 570$

**Multiply.**

1.  $\begin{array}{r}73\\\times\phantom{0}4\\\hline\end{array}$
2.  $\begin{array}{r}25\\\times\phantom{0}2\\\hline\end{array}$
3.  $\begin{array}{r}36\\\times\phantom{0}3\\\hline\end{array}$
4.  $\begin{array}{r}52\\\times\phantom{0}5\\\hline\end{array}$

5.  $\begin{array}{r}23\\\times\phantom{0}4\\\hline\end{array}$
6.  $\begin{array}{r}19\\\times\phantom{0}2\\\hline\end{array}$
7.  $\begin{array}{r}26\\\times\phantom{0}2\\\hline\end{array}$
8.  $\begin{array}{r}68\\\times\phantom{0}3\\\hline\end{array}$

9.  $\begin{array}{r}54\\\times\phantom{0}5\\\hline\end{array}$
10. $\begin{array}{r}47\\\times\phantom{0}8\\\hline\end{array}$
11. $\begin{array}{r}32\\\times\phantom{0}9\\\hline\end{array}$
12. $\begin{array}{r}48\\\times\phantom{0}8\\\hline\end{array}$

13. $\begin{array}{r}52\\\times\phantom{0}3\\\hline\end{array}$
14. $\begin{array}{r}34\\\times\phantom{0}4\\\hline\end{array}$
15. $\begin{array}{r}63\\\times\phantom{0}2\\\hline\end{array}$
16. $\begin{array}{r}55\\\times\phantom{0}3\\\hline\end{array}$

Name _____

# Lesson 4.5 Problem Solving

**Solve each problem.**

**Show your work.**

1. Mr. Ferris has a canoe rental business. Over the weekend, he rented 47 canoes. A canoe holds 3 people. If each canoe was full, how many people did Mr. Ferris rent to over the weekend?

    Mr. Ferris rented to _____ people.

2. The town pool opened on Memorial Day. On that day, 94 people showed up. The pool manager gave out 2 vouchers to each person for free snacks. How many vouchers did the pool manager give out?

    The manager gave out _____ vouchers.

3. Sami is saving up to buy a computer game. If he put 23 dollars a week in the bank, how much money will he have in 5 weeks?

    He will have $ _____.

4. The school planned for 92 students to attend the school dance. The school bought 4 slices of pizza for each student. How many slices did the school buy?

    The school bought _____ slices.

Spectrum Math Grade 4

63

Name _____

# Lesson 4.6 Multiplying 3-Digit by 1-Digit Numbers with Regrouping

To multiply 3-digit numbers by 1-digit numbers with regrouping, follow these steps.

**Step 1:**
$$\begin{array}{r} \overset{1}{6}5\overset{}{2} \\ \times\phantom{00}8 \\ \hline 6 \end{array}$$
Multiply the ones. $2 \times 8 = 16$
Put the 6 under the ones and regroup the 1 ten.

**Step 2:**
$$\begin{array}{r} \overset{4}{6}\overset{1}{5}2 \\ \times\phantom{00}8 \\ \hline 16 \end{array}$$
Multiply the tens by the ones. $50 \times 8 = 400$
Add the extra ten. $400 + 10 = 410$.
Put the 1 ten under the tens and regroup the 4 hundreds.

**Step 3:**
$$\begin{array}{r} \overset{4}{6}\overset{1}{5}2 \\ \times\phantom{00}8 \\ \hline 5,216 \end{array}$$
Multiply the hundreds by the ones. $600 \times 8 = 4,800$
Add the extra hundreds. $4,800 + 400 = 5,200$
Put the 2 under the hundreds and the 5 under the thousands.

**Multiply.**

| | a | | b | | c | | d |
|---|---|---|---|---|---|---|---|
| 1. | 118 × 3 | 2. | 305 × 4 | 3. | 224 × 5 | 4. | 152 × 3 |
| 5. | 200 × 7 | 6. | 137 × 5 | 7. | 327 × 3 | 8. | 158 × 2 |
| 9. | 235 × 6 | 10. | 142 × 9 | 11. | 580 × 3 | 12. | 129 × 9 |
| 13. | 335 × 5 | 14. | 190 × 7 | 15. | 421 × 8 | 16. | 201 × 9 |

Spectrum Math Grade 4

# Lesson 4.7 Multiplying 2-Digit by 2-Digit Numbers with Regrouping

To multiply 2-digit numbers by 2-digit numbers with regrouping, follow these steps.

**Step 1:**

$$\begin{array}{r} \overset{6}{1}9 \\ \times\ 27 \\ \hline 3 \end{array}$$

Multiply the ones.   9 × 7 = 63
Put the 3 under the ones and regroup the 6 tens.

$$\begin{array}{r} \overset{6}{1}9 \\ \times\ 27 \\ \hline 133 \end{array}$$

Multiply the tens by the ones.   10 × 7 = 70
Add the extra tens.   70 + 60 = 130
Put the 3 under the tens and the 1 under the hundreds.

**Step 2:**

$$\begin{array}{r} \overset{1}{\phantom{1}}\overset{6}{\phantom{1}} \\ 19 \\ \times\ 27 \\ \hline 133 \\ 80 \end{array}$$

Multiply the ones by tens.   9 × 20 = 180
Put the 80 under the tens and regroup the 1 hundred.

$$\begin{array}{r} \overset{1}{\phantom{1}}\overset{6}{\phantom{1}} \\ 19 \\ \times\ 27 \\ \hline 133 \\ 380 \end{array}$$

Multiply the tens by the tens.   10 × 20 = 200
Add the extra hundred.   200 + 100 = 300
Put the 3 under the hundreds.

**Step 3:**

$$\begin{array}{r} \overset{1}{\phantom{1}}\overset{6}{\phantom{1}} \\ 19 \\ \times\ 27 \\ \hline 133 \\ +380 \\ \hline 513 \end{array}$$

Add the partial products.   133 + 380 = 513

**Multiply.**

1.  22
    × 33

2.  45
    × 11

3.  80
    × 10

4.  31
    × 23

Spectrum Math Grade 4

Name _____

## Lesson 4.7 Multiplying 2-Digit by 2-Digit Numbers with Regrouping

**Multiply.**

1. 22
   × 19

2. 52
   × 48

3. 28
   × 25

4. 77
   × 30

5. 33
   × 29

6. 57
   × 23

7. 65
   × 17

8. 88
   × 22

9. 91
   × 38

10. 55
    × 17

11. 44
    × 23

12. 88
    × 17

Can you multiply 5,400 by 1,200 using only 2-digit numbers? Try it!

Name _____

# Lesson 4.8 Multiplying 3-Digit by 2-Digit Numbers with Regrouping

**Multiply.**

1. 315
   × 30

2. 527
   × 42

3. 287
   × 21

4. 209
   × 30

5. 813
   × 17

6. 140
   × 32

7. 196
   × 23

8. 673
   × 92

9. 542
   × 48

10. 604
    × 40

11. 713
    × 67

12. 900
    × 42

13. 198
    × 71

14. 513
    × 58

15. 841
    × 71

16. 482
    × 63

Spectrum Math Grade 4

67

Name _____

# Lesson 4.9 Multiplying 4-Digit by 1-Digit Numbers with Regrouping

To multiply 4-digit numbers by 1-digit numbers with regrouping, follow these steps.

**Step 1:**
$$\begin{array}{r} \overset{2}{8,20}8 \\ \times \phantom{000}3 \\ \hline 4 \end{array}$$
Multiply the ones. $8 \times 3 = 24$
Put the 4 ones under the ones and regroup the 2 tens.

**Step 2:**
$$\begin{array}{r} \overset{2}{8,20}8 \\ \times \phantom{000}3 \\ \hline 24 \end{array}$$
Multiply the tens by ones. $0 \times 3 = 0$
Add the extra tens. $0 + 20 = 20$
Put the 2 tens under the tens.

**Step 3:**
$$\begin{array}{r} \overset{2}{8,20}8 \\ \times \phantom{000}3 \\ \hline 624 \end{array}$$
Multiply the hundreds by ones. $200 \times 3 = 600$
Put the 6 hundreds under the hundreds.

**Step 4:**
$$\begin{array}{r} \overset{2}{8,20}8 \\ \times \phantom{000}3 \\ \hline 24,624 \end{array}$$
Multiply the thousands by ones. $8,000 \times 3 = 24,000$
Put the 24 thousands under the thousands.

**Multiply.**

| | a | b | c | d |
|---|---|---|---|---|
| 1. | 4,395 × 7 | 2. 7,096 × 5 | 3. 3,054 × 2 | 4. 5,321 × 5 |
| 5. | 9,443 × 2 | 6. 6,356 × 5 | 7. 7,553 × 3 | 8. 5,448 × 8 |
| 9. | 2,209 × 5 | 10. 8,115 × 6 | 11. 6,478 × 2 | 12. 2,910 × 9 |

Spectrum Math Grade 4
68

Name _____

# Lesson 4.10 Problem Solving

**Solve each problem.**

**Show your work.**

1. Zach loves pears. He ate 2 pears each day for 48 days. How many pears did Zach eat in all?

   Zach ate _____ pears.

2. Claudia breeds pet mice. If her 12 female mice have 33 babies each, how many baby mice will Claudia have in all?

   Claudia will have _____ baby mice.

3. In a tropical rainforest, the average annual rainfall is 150 inches. After 5 years, how much rain will have fallen in the rainforest?

   _____ inches of rain will have fallen.

4. Buses were reserved for the big field trip. If each bus holds 40 students, how many students would 6 buses hold?

   The buses would hold _____ students.

Spectrum Math Grade 4

Name _____

**Posttest** Chapter 4

**Multiply.**

1.  72
    × 4

2.  24
    × 8

3.  399
    × 2

4.  242
    × 3

5.  643
    × 7

6.  3,417
    × 7

7.  2,981
    × 6

8.  5,350
    × 4

9.  75
    × 64

10. 17
    × 23

11. 816
    × 13

12. 262
    × 24

**Write the factors of each number. Then, label it *prime* or *composite*.**

| | Factors | Prime or Composite |
|---|---|---|
| 13. 85 | _____ | _____ |
| 14. 59 | _____ | _____ |
| 15. 15 | _____ | _____ |
| 16. 26 | _____ | _____ |
| 17. 70 | _____ | _____ |
| 18. 34 | _____ | _____ |

Spectrum Math Grade 4

Name _____

# Posttest Chapter 4

**Solve each problem.**  **Show your work.**

**19.** A community center loaned 12 schools a set of 21 laptops each. How many laptops did they loan in all?

The center loaned _____ laptops.

**20.** A girls' club is trying to get into the record book for the most braids done in a day. If there are 372 girls and each completes 40 braids, then how many braids will they have done?

They will have done _____ braids.

**21.** Mrs. Nance's science class raised tadpoles. If 35 students raised 23 tadpoles each, how many tadpoles did the class raise in all?

The class raised _____ tadpoles in all.

**22.** In the Lakeside View homesite, 15 apartment buildings were constructed. If there are 12 units in each building, how many units were constructed?

_____ units were constructed.

Spectrum Math Grade 4

# Chapter 5: Division

## Helpful Definitions

**dividend**: the number being divided
**divisor**: the number the dividend is being divided by
**quotient**: the answer to a division problem

$$\text{divisor} \rightarrow 8\overline{)48} \leftarrow \text{dividend}$$
$$\phantom{\text{divisor} \rightarrow 8\overline{)}}6 \leftarrow \text{quotient}$$

**multiple**: the product of a given number and any other number, or more simply the numbers you say when you skip count by a number
      Multiples of 10: 10, 20, 30, 40, 50, . . .
      Multiples of 2: 2, 4, 6, 8, 10, 12, . . .

**remainder**: an amount left over after dividing a number that cannot be divided into equal groups

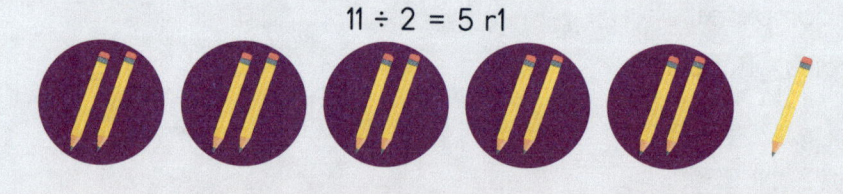

$$11 \div 2 = 5 \text{ r}1$$

There are 5 equal groups of 2 pencils. There is one pencil left over. The remainder is 1.

## Skills Checklist

☐ Dividing multiples of 10 and 100

☐ Using knowledge of multiplication facts to divide

☐ Solving word problems using division

☐ Dividing up to four-digit numbers with and without remainders

## Tools and Tips

People use division often in their daily lives to share or to put items into equal groups. When your student has a solid understanding of division, they will be able to divide items into equal groups. For example, your student may wish to divide 15 strawberries into 3 equal groups to share with friends.

Help your student understand that multiplication and division are related. For example, show them a multiplication problem using small items around your home. You can use crayons, small toys, or pieces of cereal. For 4 × 5 = 20, you can show your student 4 groups of items with 5 items in each group. Then, relate the items to the problem 20 ÷ 5 = 4. Using real items to show the problems will help your student have a clear understanding of multiplication facts and how they relate to division facts.

Help your student understand that ÷ and $\overline{)}$ mean the same thing by having them use both symbols. Write a multiplication fact, such as 5 × 6 = 30. Have your student write the related division facts that go with the multiplication fact. Have them write the fact two ways, using each symbol:

$$30 \div 6 = 5 \text{ and } 6\overline{)30}^{\,5}$$

As your student becomes fluent in multiplication and division facts, they will be able to perform more complicated problems. There are a variety of strategies to help visualize division problems. Your student could try an area model or the partial quotients method.

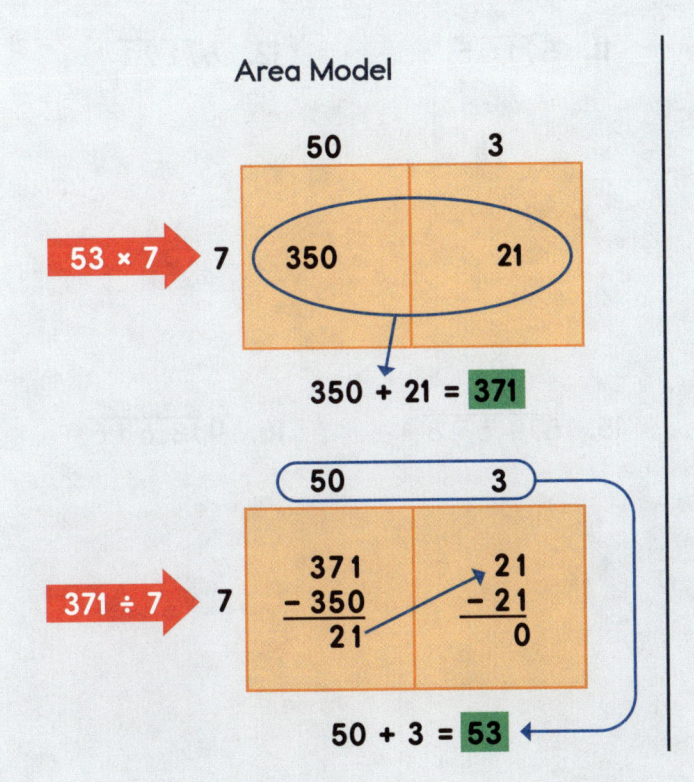

### Area Model

53 × 7

|   | 50 | 3 |
|---|----|---|
| 7 | 350 | 21 |

350 + 21 = **371**

371 ÷ 7

|   | 50 | 3 |
|---|----|---|
| 7 | 371<br>− 350<br>21 | 21<br>− 21<br>0 |

50 + 3 = **53**

### Partial Quotients

```
      65 r6              same      65 r6
   8)526                answer!  8)526
    − 80  10                     −400  50
     446                          126
    − 80  10                     − 80  10
     366                           46
    − 80  10                     − 40   5
     286                            6  65
    − 80  10
     206
    − 80  10
     126
    − 80  10
      46
    − 40   5
       6  65
```

Spectrum Math Grade 4

Name _____

**Pretest** Chapter 5

Divide.

1. 3)15  2. 7)49  3. 9)27  4. 5)45

5. 6)30  6. 3)18  7. 7)42  8. 9)81

9. 7)56  10. 3)30  11. 5)105  12. 6)121

13. 3)900  14. 5)2,214  15. 5)4,693  16. 4)8,616

Name _____

# Pretest Chapter 5

**Solve each problem.**   Show your work.

17. The Pancake Restaurant served 32 pancakes. If 8 customers ate an equal number of pancakes, how many did each person eat?

    Each person ate _____ pancakes.

18. The drama club is giving a party in the school lunchroom. The club wants to be seated in groups of 8. If 64 students go to the party, how many groups of students will there be?

    There will be _____ groups of students.

19. The school spirit club baked cakes for a charity event. There were 75 different cakes and 5 bakers. Each baker baked the same number of cakes. How many cakes did each baker make?

    Each baker made _____ cakes.

20. The glee club needs to sell 376 tickets to win a trip. If there are 8 members who want to go on the trip, how many tickets does each member need to sell?

    Each member needs to sell _____ tickets.

Spectrum Math Grade 4

Name _____

## Lesson 5.1 Dividing Multiples of 10 and 100

We can use place value to help divide by multiples of ten and hundred.

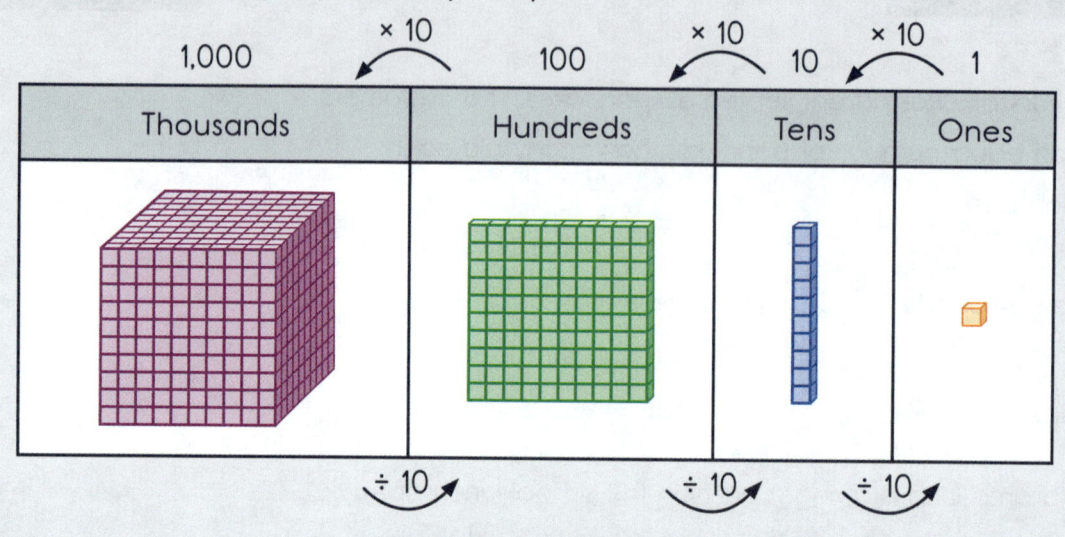

| Thousands | Hundreds | Tens | Ones |
|---|---|---|---|

1,000 ×10→ 100 ×10→ 10 ×10→ 1

←÷10  ←÷10  ←÷10

4,000 ÷ 40 = ?

$\frac{4,000}{4} \div \frac{40}{4}$ = 1,000 ÷ 10 = 100

900 ÷ 10 = ?

$\frac{900}{10} \div \frac{10}{10}$ = 90 ÷ 1 = 90

**Divide.**

1. 300 ÷ 3 = _____

2. 60 ÷ 6 = _____

3. 100 ÷ 10 = _____

4. 200 ÷ 20 = _____

5. 800 ÷ 80 = _____

6. 700 ÷ 7 = _____

7. 9,000 ÷ 90 = _____

8. 400 ÷ 40 = _____

9. 600 ÷ 10 = _____

10. 40 ÷ 10 = _____

11. 200 ÷ 10 = _____

12. 90 ÷ 10 = _____

Name _____

# Lesson 5.2 Dividing through 45 ÷ 5

divisor → 5)4̄5̄ ← dividend, quotient = 9

To check your answer, do the inverse operation.
If 45 ÷ 5 = 9, then 5 × 9 = 45 must be true.

Using the multiplication table, find 45 in the 5 column. The quotient is named at the beginning of the row.

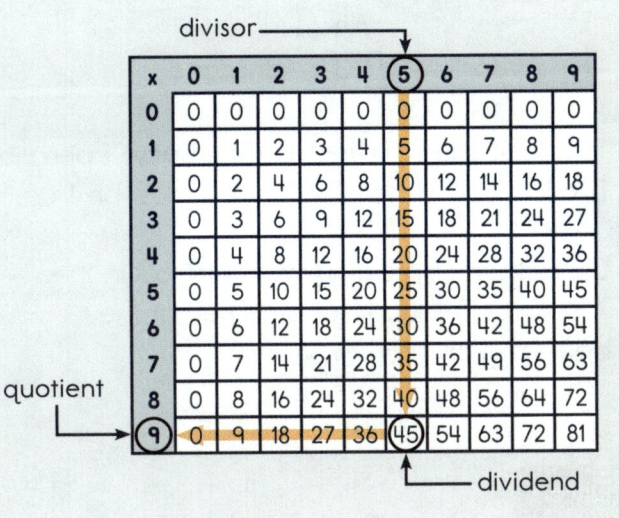

**Divide.**

1. 5)35    2. 4)16    3. 4)36    4. 3)18    5. 5)25

6. 2)18    7. 3)15    8. 5)20    9. 3)27    10. 5)45

11. 4)32   12. 5)40   13. 7)35   14. 4)24   15. 5)35

Explain how you would use multiplication to check the division problem 3)15.

_____

_____

Spectrum Math Grade 4

77

Name _____

## Lesson 5.3 Dividing through 63 ÷ 7

divisor ⟶ 7)$\overline{63}$ ⟵ dividend, with 9 ⟵ quotient

To check your answer, do the inverse operation.
If 63 ÷ 7 = 9, then 7 × 9 = 63 must be true.

Using the multiplication table, find 63 in the 7 column. The quotient is named at the beginning of the row.

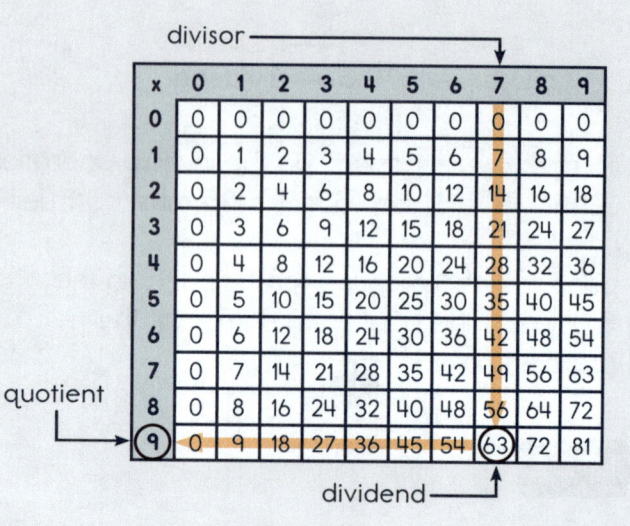

| x | 0 | 1 | 2 | 3 | 4 | 5 | 6 | 7 | 8 | 9 |
|---|---|---|---|---|---|---|---|---|---|---|
| 0 | 0 | 0 | 0 | 0 | 0 | 0 | 0 | 0 | 0 | 0 |
| 1 | 0 | 1 | 2 | 3 | 4 | 5 | 6 | 7 | 8 | 9 |
| 2 | 0 | 2 | 4 | 6 | 8 | 10 | 12 | 14 | 16 | 18 |
| 3 | 0 | 3 | 6 | 9 | 12 | 15 | 18 | 21 | 24 | 27 |
| 4 | 0 | 4 | 8 | 12 | 16 | 20 | 24 | 28 | 32 | 36 |
| 5 | 0 | 5 | 10 | 15 | 20 | 25 | 30 | 35 | 40 | 45 |
| 6 | 0 | 6 | 12 | 18 | 24 | 30 | 36 | 42 | 48 | 54 |
| 7 | 0 | 7 | 14 | 21 | 28 | 35 | 42 | 49 | 56 | 63 |
| 8 | 0 | 8 | 16 | 24 | 32 | 40 | 48 | 56 | 64 | 72 |
| 9 | 0 | 9 | 18 | 27 | 36 | 45 | 54 | 63 | 72 | 81 |

### Divide.

1. 7)$\overline{49}$
2. 9)$\overline{45}$
3. 6)$\overline{36}$
4. 3)$\overline{24}$
5. 4)$\overline{28}$

6. 2)$\overline{20}$
7. 4)$\overline{24}$
8. 4)$\overline{32}$
9. 5)$\overline{45}$
10. 2)$\overline{16}$

11. 5)$\overline{40}$
12. 7)$\overline{42}$
13. 6)$\overline{12}$
14. 5)$\overline{35}$
15. 7)$\overline{56}$

Can you write an inverse of 42 ÷ 7 = 6? Try it!

_____

Name _____

# Lesson 5.4 Dividing through 81 ÷ 9

$$\text{divisor} \rightarrow 9\overline{)81} \leftarrow \text{dividend}$$
quotient → 9

To check your answer, do the inverse operation.
If 81 ÷ 9 = 9, then 9 × 9 = 81 must be true.

Using the multiplication table, find 81 in the 9 column. The quotient is named at the beginning of the row.

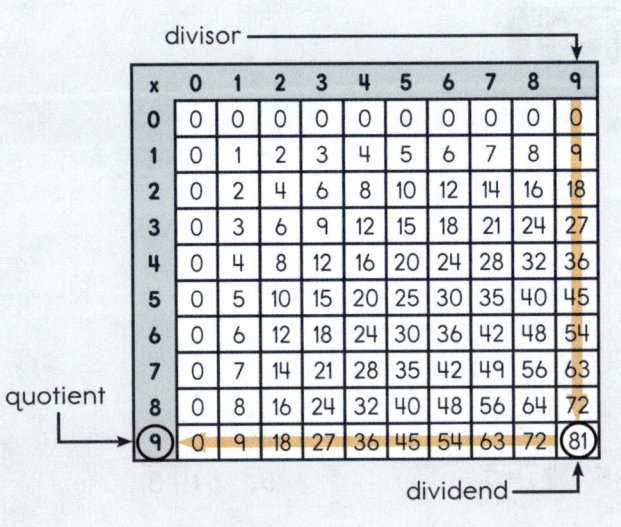

| x | 0 | 1 | 2 | 3 | 4 | 5 | 6 | 7 | 8 | 9 |
|---|---|---|---|---|---|---|---|---|---|---|
| 0 | 0 | 0 | 0 | 0 | 0 | 0 | 0 | 0 | 0 | 0 |
| 1 | 0 | 1 | 2 | 3 | 4 | 5 | 6 | 7 | 8 | 9 |
| 2 | 0 | 2 | 4 | 6 | 8 | 10 | 12 | 14 | 16 | 18 |
| 3 | 0 | 3 | 6 | 9 | 12 | 15 | 18 | 21 | 24 | 27 |
| 4 | 0 | 4 | 8 | 12 | 16 | 20 | 24 | 28 | 32 | 36 |
| 5 | 0 | 5 | 10 | 15 | 20 | 25 | 30 | 35 | 40 | 45 |
| 6 | 0 | 6 | 12 | 18 | 24 | 30 | 36 | 42 | 48 | 54 |
| 7 | 0 | 7 | 14 | 21 | 28 | 35 | 42 | 49 | 56 | 63 |
| 8 | 0 | 8 | 16 | 24 | 32 | 40 | 48 | 56 | 64 | 72 |
| 9 | 0 | 9 | 18 | 27 | 36 | 45 | 54 | 63 | 72 | 81 |

**Divide.**

1. 9)72    2. 8)40    3. 8)24    4. 6)48    5. 7)28

6. 6)36    7. 3)21    8. 7)49    9. 9)54    10. 8)64

11. 9)45    12. 8)48    13. 7)14    14. 9)36    15. 4)28

Spectrum Math Grade 4

Name _____

## Lesson 5.5 Division Practice

**Divide.**

1. 8)56
2. 6)24
3. 2)18
4. 5)35

5. 7)42
6. 6)48
7. 5)30
8. 8)72

9. 3)12
10. 9)81
11. 9)54
12. 3)21

13. 7)63
14. 3)24
15. 5)40
16. 4)16

17. 9)27
18. 7)49
19. 8)64
20. 9)36

Name _____

# Lesson 5.6 Problem Solving

**Solve each problem.**  **Show your work.**

1. Eddie and Toru listened to 72 of their favorite songs. If there were 9 songs on each album, how many albums did they listen to?

   They listened to _____ albums.

2. Ms. Ruiz printed 35 tests for her students. If there were 7 equal rows of students, how many tests were passed out to each row?

   There were _____ tests passed out to each row.

3. Gary opened a bag of candy containing 81 pieces. He wants to give each of his guests the same number of pieces. If he has 9 guests, how many pieces does each person get?

   Each guest gets _____ pieces.

4. The warehouse has 63 boxes of cat litter. The same number of boxes will be sent to 9 stores. How many boxes will each store get?

   Each store will get _____ boxes.

Spectrum Math Grade 4

Name _____

## Lesson 5.7 Dividing 2 Digits by 1 Digit

To divide a 2-digit number, use what you know about multiples and factors.

33 ÷ 8    Think: How many times does 8 go into 33?
Look at the multiples of 8: 8, 16, 24, 32, 40, . . .
8, 16, 24, 32, 40    Think: Which multiple is close to 33 without being greater than 33? (32)
So, because 32 ÷ 8 = 4, 33 ÷ 8 is between 4 and 5.

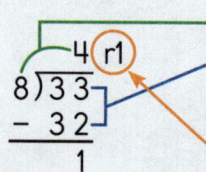

```
   4 r1
8)33        8 × 4 = 32
 -32        Subtract.
   1        Because 33 − 32 = 1 and 1 is less than 8, the remainder is recorded like this.
```

**Divide.**

1. 5)26    2. 7)57    3. 4)31    4. 9)81

5. 6)35    6. 8)66    7. 3)17    8. 2)13

9. 7)50    10. 6)40    11. 9)30    12. 5)41

13. 3)10    14. 8)73    15. 7)57    16. 8)20

82                                                           Spectrum Math Grade 4

# Lesson 5.7 Dividing 2 Digits by 1 Digit

To divide a 2-digit number, use what you know about multiples and factors.

31 ÷ 3         Think: How many times does 3 go into 31?
               Look at the multiples of 3: 3, 6, 9, 12, 15, 18, 21, 24, 27, 30, 33, . . .
3, 6, 9, 12, 15, 18,   Think: Which multiple is close to 31 without being greater than 31? (30)
21, 24, 27, 30, 33, . . .  So, because 30 ÷ 3 = 10, 31 ÷ 3 is between 10 and 11.

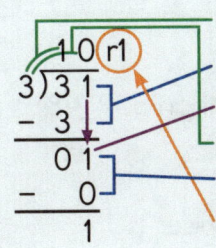

```
    10 r1
3)3 1       3 × 1 = 3
 - 3         Subtract.
   0 1       Bring down the 1.
  - 0        3 × 0 = 0
     1       Subtract.
```
Because 1 − 0 = 1 and 1 is less than 3, the remainder is recorded like this.

**Divide.**

1. 2)36        2. 5)76        3. 4)79        4. 4)96

5. 5)86        6. 3)96        7. 8)99        8. 7)84

9. 6)93        10. 8)89       11. 4)88       12. 4)78

13. 8)93       14. 3)75       15. 9)99       16. 7)93

Spectrum Math Grade 4

Name _____

## Lesson 5.8 Dividing 3 Digits by 1 Digit

To divide a 3-digit number, use what you know about multiples and factors.

453 ÷ 8

```
    56 r5
 8)453
  -40
    53
   -48
     5
```

Think: How many times does 8 go into 45?
Look at the multiples of 8: 8, 16, 24, 32, 40, 48, . . .
Think: Which multiple is closest to 45 but not greater than 45? (40)
8 × 5 = 40
Subtract. Bring down the 3.
Think: How many times does 8 go into 53?
Look at the multiples of 8: 8, 16, 24, 32, 40, 48, 56, . . .
Think: Which multiple is closest to 53 but not greater than 53? (48)
8 × 6 = 48
Subtract.
Because 53 − 48 = 5 and 5 is less than 8, the remainder is recorded like this.

**Divide.**

1. 8)720      2. 4)327      3. 9)372      4. 4)173

5. 6)552      6. 3)139      7. 4)248      8. 9)980

84

Spectrum Math Grade 4

Name _____

**Lesson 5.8** Dividing 3 Digits by 1 Digit

Divide.

1. 6)773
2. 2)898
3. 4)566
4. 6)781

5. 2)317
6. 4)732
7. 9)989
8. 7)897

9. 3)972
10. 2)394
11. 5)529
12. 8)897

13. 3)784
14. 5)788
15. 3)676
16. 2)348

Name _____

## Lesson 5.9 Dividing 4 Digits by 1 Digit

Solve 8,917 ÷ 4.

```
      2              2 2            2 2 2          2,2 2 9 r1
   4)8,917        4)8,917        4)8,917        4)8,917
    -8↓            -8↓             -8↓             -8↓
     09             09              09              09
                   -8↓             -8↓             -8↓
                    11              11              11
                                   -8↓             -8↓
                                    37              37
                                                   -36
                                                     1
```

**Divide.**

1. 2)2,612    2. 5)8,603    3. 4)8,263    4. 7)6,137

5. 6)6,219    6. 2)4,921    7. 8)9,061    8. 3)6,363

86

Spectrum Math Grade 4

Name _____

## Lesson 5.9 Dividing 4 Digits by 1 Digit

Solve 2,142 ÷ 6.

```
      3              3 5             3 5 7
  6)2,142        6)2,142         6)2,142
   -1 8↓          -1 8↓            -1 8↓
     3 4            3 4              3 4
                   -3 0↓             -3 0↓
                     4 2               4 2
                                      -4 2
                                         0
```

**Divide.**

1. 4)4,783    2. 4)1,207    3. 5)3,901    4. 2)9,131

5. 5)3,197    6. 2)6,641    7. 7)3,440    8. 3)8,421

9. 8)4,304    10. 2)2,528    11. 3)7,293    12. 5)6,365

Spectrum Math Grade 4

87

Name _____

## Lesson 5.10 Problem Solving

**Solve each problem.**  **Show your work.**

1. Ms. Garrett had 40 guests at her birthday party. She cut her cake into 88 slices. Each guest ate 2 slices of cake. How many slices were left?

   There were _____ slices left.

2. Lucy babysits for 2 families. She works the same number of hours each month for each family. If she worked 76 hours last month, how many hours did she work for each family?

   She worked _____ hours for each family.

3. An afterschool club ate 210 sleeves of crackers. Each box contains 4 sleeves of crackers. How many boxes did they open? How many sleeves of crackers are left?

   They opened _____ boxes of crackers.

   There are _____ sleeves of crackers left.

4. The school supply store received a shipment of 3,650 pens. If the pens are packed in 5 boxes, how many pens are in each box?

   There are _____ pens in each box.

Name _____

# Lesson 5.10 Problem Solving

**Solve each problem.**  **Show your work.**

1. The garden show is moving into a bigger area. The new space has 935 square feet of space for displays. There are 8 different displays, and each display will need the same amount of space. How many square feet does each display get? How many square feet are left over?

   Each display gets _____ square feet of space.

   There are _____ square feet of space left over.

2. Taylor needs 612 more dollars to buy a plane ticket to visit his cousin in Alabama. If he saves 9 dollars a day, how soon can he go to Alabama?

   He will have the rest of the money in _____ days.

3. The bait shop ordered 136 worms for their customers. The workers put them into 8 separate cups. How many worms are in each cup?

   There are _____ worms in each cup.

Spectrum Math Grade 4

89

Name _____

**Posttest** Chapter 5

Divide.

1. 3)18     2. 9)27     3. 8)64     4. 4)40

5. 9)72     6. 6)36     7. 8)16     8. 7)21

9. 5)25     10. 8)34    11. 9)54    12. 5)35

13. 2)96    14. 3)87    15. 8)93    16. 7)31

17. 5)917   18. 6)762   19. 30)3,000   20. 3)6,118

Name _____

**Posttest** Chapter 5

**Solve each problem.**    Show your work.

21. A group of 7 teenagers cut lawns over the weekend. They made 56 dollars. Each teen will make the same amount. How much money will each teen get?

    Each teen will get _____ dollars.

22. Gloria decided to make lemonade for her family. There are 8 people in her family. The pitcher will hold 24 glasses of lemonade. How many glasses can each person have?

    Each person can have _____ glasses.

23. Susan, Marta, and Aisha have 5 hours to spend at the zoo. There are 40 different animals they want to see. During each hour at the zoo, how many animals should they plan to see?

    They should plan to see _____ different animals each hour.

24. At baseball practice, 325 pitches were thrown to the players. If 5 players got the same number of pitches, how many pitches did each player get?

    Each player got _____ pitches.

Spectrum Math Grade 4

Name _____

# Learning Checkpoint Chapters 1–5

**Add or subtract.**

1.  14
   + 5

2.  73
   + 1

3.  80
   + 9

4.  52
   + 7

5.  32
   − 1

6.  76
   − 5

7.  25
   − 15

8.  87
   − 34

9.  74
   − 8

10. 93
    − 9

11. 17
    − 9

12. 38
    − 19

13. 52
    + 17

14. 32
    17
    + 10

15. 43
    21
    + 18

16. 73
    + 26

17. 320
    − 18

18. 715
    − 23

19. 287
    − 78

20. 408
    − 19

Name _____

## Learning Checkpoint Chapters 1–5

**Write each number in expanded form.**

**21.** 732 _____

**22.** 64,100 _____

**23.** 4,790 _____

**24.** 1,003 _____

**25.** 314,732 _____

**26.** 50,020 _____

**Round each number to the place named.**

**27.** hundreds: 13,573     **28.** ten thousands: 75,319     **29.** thousands: 932,710

_____              _____              _____

**Compare each pair of numbers. Write >, <, or =.**

**30.** 13,702 ◯ 13,207     **31.** 3,976 ◯ 9,362     **32.** 26,314 ◯ 260,314

**33.** 978 ◯ 978     **34.** 721,460 ◯ 710,460     **35.** 8,402 ◯ 4,820

Spectrum Math Grade 4

Name _____

# Learning Checkpoint Chapters 1–5

**Add.**

| | | | | | | | | |
|---|---|---|---|---|---|---|---|---|
| 36. | 703<br>+ 172 | 37. | 665<br>+ 118 | 38. | 6,511<br>+ 1,430 | 39. | 2,314<br>+ 718 |

**Subtract.**

| | | | | | | | | |
|---|---|---|---|---|---|---|---|---|
| 40. | 32,146<br>− 3,132 | 41. | 42,804<br>− 38,709 | 42. | 34,932<br>− 17,983 | 43. | 39,702<br>− 615 |

**Add.**

| | | | | | | | | |
|---|---|---|---|---|---|---|---|---|
| 44. | 4,132<br>714<br>+ 304 | 45. | 8,215<br>1,730<br>+ 1,045 | 46. | 3,014<br>1,246<br>+ 710 | 47. | 7,300<br>715<br>243<br>+ 120 |

| | | | | | | | | |
|---|---|---|---|---|---|---|---|---|
| 48. | 83,548<br>+ 8,162 | 49. | 108,765<br>+ 2,046 | 50. | 45,059<br>+ 38,712 | 51. | 71,042<br>+ 8,925 |

94  Spectrum Math Grade 4

# Learning Checkpoint Chapters 1–5

**Multiply.**

52.  7
    × 8

53.  9
    × 4

54.  7
    × 4

55.  8
    × 6

56.  2 1
    ×   4

57.  3 2
    ×   8

58.  1 4
    ×   2

59.  4 4
    ×   2

60.  1 2
    ×   4

61.  2 0
    ×   4

62.  4 8
    ×   7

63.  7 2
    ×   8

64.  8 4
    ×   5

65.  2 5
    ×   7

66.  4 9
    ×   9

67.  1 1
    × 1 0

68.  2 2
    × 1 1

69.  3 1
    × 3 2

70.  4 3
    × 2 0

71.  5 0
    × 1 0

Spectrum Math Grade 4

95

# Learning Checkpoint Chapters 1–5

**Multiply.**

72.  41 × 20

73.  75 × 25

74.  32 × 18

75.  81 × 37

76.  68 × 30

77.  418 × 45

78.  500 × 32

79.  199 × 47

80.  578 × 23

81.  887 × 52

**Divide.**

82.  9)81

83.  7)56

84.  6)48

85.  8)64

86.  7)42

87.  3)300

88.  2)642

89.  7)721

Name _____

# Learning Checkpoint Chapters 1–5

**Solve each problem.**  **Show your work.**

**90.** A total of 68 hikers went on a trip to Blue Hill Mountain. If 32 of the hikers were adults, how many hikers were children?

_____ hikers were children.

**91.** On a trip to Washington, DC, there were 33 fifth-graders and 27 fourth-graders. How many students were on the trip?

There were _____ students on the trip.

**92.** At the park, bird watchers saw 42 robins looking for worms. If there were 5 times as many starlings as robins, how many starlings were there?

There were _____ starlings.

**93.** A group of friends is getting ready for a hike at night. Each of their flashlights take 4 batteries. If they have 72 batteries, how many flashlights can they take?

They can take _____ flashlights.

Spectrum Math Grade 4

97

## Chapter 6: Fractions

### Helpful Definitions

**numerator:** part of the whole
**denominator:** parts in all

$\dfrac{8}{10}$ ← numerator (part of the whole)
← denominator (parts in all)

**equivalent fractions:** fractions that have the same value but different numerators and denominators; for example, $\dfrac{4}{5}$ and $\dfrac{8}{10}$ are equivalent

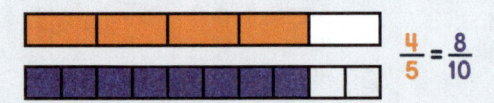

$\dfrac{4}{5} = \dfrac{8}{10}$

**mixed number (mixed numeral):** a combination of a whole number and fraction; for example, $3\dfrac{1}{4}$ means three wholes and 1 part out of 4

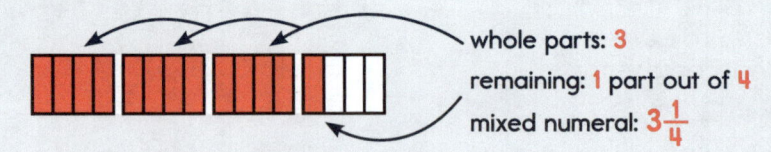

whole parts: 3
remaining: 1 part out of 4
mixed numeral: $3\dfrac{1}{4}$

**simplest form:** the form a fraction is in when you cannot divide the numerator and denominator any further by the same number and still have whole numbers.

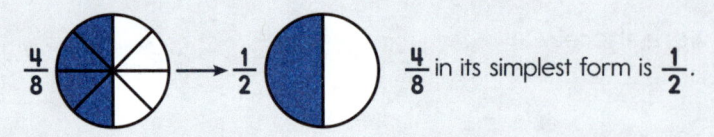

$\dfrac{4}{8} \rightarrow \dfrac{1}{2}$    $\dfrac{4}{8}$ in its simplest form is $\dfrac{1}{2}$.

**decompose:** to divide a fraction into the smaller parts that make up the fraction

**least common multiple:** the smallest multiple that two numbers have in common
Multiples of 3: 3, 6, 9, ⑫, 15, 18, 21, 24, . . .
Multiples of 4: 4, 8, ⑫, 16, 20, 24, 28, 32, . . .
The numbers 3 and 4 have common multiples of 12 and 24. However, 12 is the least common multiple between the numbers.

98    Spectrum Math Grade 4

## Skills Checklist

☐ Creating equivalent fractions

☐ Creating like (common) denominators

☐ Comparing fractions

☐ Adding and subtracting fractions and mixed numbers

☐ Decomposing fractions

☐ Multiplying fractions by whole numbers

☐ Changing fractions to decimals

☐ Comparing two decimals

## Tools and Tips

Fractions are all around us and in our daily lives. They are used in recipes, measurement, and in sharing items equally with friends and family. When your student understands fractions, they will be able to use them in real-world situations and in more complex mathematical concepts in the coming years.

Your student needs to be able to create equivalent, or equal, fractions. For example, $\frac{1}{2}$ and $\frac{4}{8}$ are equivalent fractions. Equivalent fractions are necessary in order to compare, add, and subtract fractions. You can help your student understand fractions by pointing them out in your everyday lives. For example, a pizza may have 8 slices. Note that 1 slice is $\frac{1}{8}$ of the pizza. Ask your student to name the fraction for half of the pizza: $\frac{4}{8}$ or $\frac{1}{2}$. Explain that these are equivalent fractions because they represent the same value or size of pizza.

Spectrum Math Grade 4

Name _____

**Pretest** Chapter 6

To find an equivalent fraction, multiply both numerator and denominator by the number in the circle.

1. $\frac{3}{6}$ = _____ ④

2. $\frac{2}{3}$ = _____ ⑤

3. $\frac{1}{6}$ = _____ ⑥

4. $\frac{1}{3}$ = _____ ⑨

Draw a picture to compare the fractions. Then, write >, <, or =.

5. $\frac{1}{5}$ ○ $\frac{2}{10}$

6. $\frac{3}{4}$ ○ $\frac{5}{8}$

Add or subtract.

7. $\frac{7}{10} + \frac{3}{10}$ = _____

8. $\frac{3}{8} + \frac{4}{8}$ = _____

9. $\frac{4}{5} - \frac{2}{5}$ = _____

10. $\frac{11}{12} - \frac{8}{12}$ = _____

Decompose the fraction.

11. $\frac{2}{4}$  □/□ + □/□  or  _____ × □/□

Write the decimal and fraction for each model.

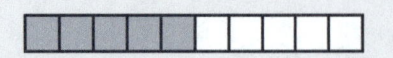

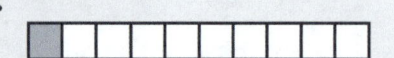

12. _____ or _____

13. _____ or _____

14. _____ or _____

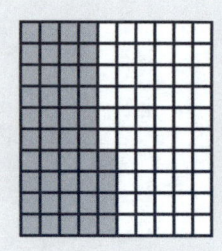

100

Spectrum Math Grade 4

Name _____

## Pretest Chapter 6

**Add or subtract.**

15. $\frac{4}{10} + \frac{8}{100} =$ _____

16. $7\frac{1}{6} + 3\frac{1}{6} =$ _____

17. $5\frac{3}{8} + 8\frac{3}{8} =$ _____

18. $8\frac{3}{5} + 8\frac{1}{5} =$ _____

19. $7\frac{7}{9} - 4\frac{4}{9} =$ _____

20. $\frac{2}{10} + \frac{2}{100} =$ _____

21. $9\frac{3}{10} + 2\frac{9}{10} =$ _____

22. $4\frac{5}{8} - 1\frac{2}{7} =$ _____

23. $3\frac{8}{10} - 2\frac{1}{5} =$ _____

**Multiply.**

24. $\frac{8}{9} \times 4 =$ _____

25. $3 \times \frac{1}{8} =$ _____

26. $\frac{4}{7} \times 2 =$ _____

27. $\frac{5}{7} \times 8 =$ _____

28. $5 \times \frac{3}{10} =$ _____

29. $2 \times \frac{7}{12} =$ _____

30. $\frac{6}{11} \times 7 =$ _____

31. $\frac{2}{9} \times 8 =$ _____

32. $4 \times \frac{3}{7} =$ _____

Spectrum Math Grade 4

Name _____

# Lesson 6.1 Finding Equivalent Fractions

To find an equivalent fraction, multiply both the numerator and denominator by the same number.

$\frac{3}{4} = \frac{3 \times 3}{4 \times 3} = \frac{9}{12}$ ← Multiply the numerator by 3.
← Multiply the denominator by 3.

$\frac{3}{4} = \frac{9}{12}$     $\frac{3}{4}$ and $\frac{9}{12}$ are equivalent fractions.

**To find an equivalent fraction, multiply the numerator and the denominator by the number in the circle.**

1. $\frac{3}{4} = $ _____ ②
2. $\frac{1}{4} = $ _____ ④
3. $\frac{2}{3} = $ _____ ⑤

4. $\frac{1}{2} = $ _____ ②
5. $\frac{1}{3} = $ _____ ⑥
6. $\frac{3}{12} = $ _____ ④

7. $\frac{5}{7} = $ _____ ②
8. $\frac{3}{6} = $ _____ ④
9. $\frac{2}{8} = $ _____ ④

10. $\frac{1}{6} = $ _____ ⑥
11. $\frac{1}{3} = $ _____ ⑨
12. $\frac{2}{3} = $ _____ ⑥

**Use multiplication to find each equivalent fraction.**

13. $\frac{1}{5} = \frac{3}{\phantom{0}}$
14. $\frac{1}{10} = \frac{\phantom{0}}{20}$
15. $\frac{3}{4} = \frac{9}{\phantom{0}}$
16. $\frac{1}{2} = \frac{9}{\phantom{0}}$

17. $\frac{1}{3} = \frac{\phantom{0}}{12}$
18. $\frac{2}{4} = \frac{8}{\phantom{0}}$
19. $\frac{1}{12} = \frac{2}{\phantom{0}}$
20. $\frac{2}{6} = \frac{\phantom{0}}{18}$

**Name** _____

# Lesson 6.2 Comparing Fractions Using Models

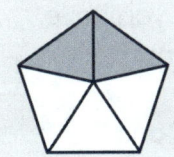

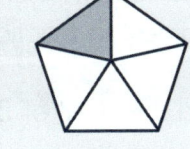

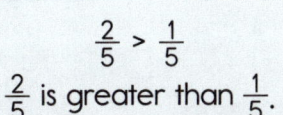

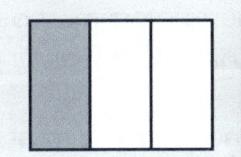

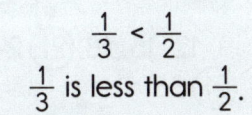

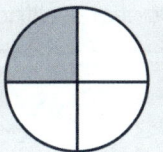

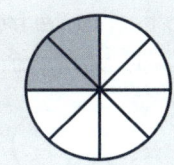

$\frac{2}{5} > \frac{1}{5}$

$\frac{2}{5}$ is greater than $\frac{1}{5}$.

$\frac{1}{3} < \frac{1}{2}$

$\frac{1}{3}$ is less than $\frac{1}{2}$.

$\frac{1}{4} = \frac{2}{8}$

$\frac{1}{4}$ is equal to $\frac{2}{8}$.

**Draw a picture to compare the fractions. Then, write >, <, or =.**

1. $\frac{1}{4}$ ◯ $\frac{3}{4}$

2. $\frac{1}{2}$ ◯ $\frac{2}{4}$

3. $\frac{2}{3}$ ◯ $\frac{1}{2}$

4. $\frac{7}{10}$ ◯ $\frac{3}{5}$

5. $\frac{3}{8}$ ◯ $\frac{3}{4}$

6. $\frac{1}{3}$ ◯ $\frac{5}{8}$

7. $\frac{1}{5}$ ◯ $\frac{2}{10}$

8. $\frac{3}{4}$ ◯ $\frac{1}{2}$

9. $\frac{6}{10}$ ◯ $\frac{2}{5}$

Spectrum Math Grade 4

# Lesson 6.3 Comparing Fractions Using the LCM

To compare fractions without pictures, the denominators must be the same. When you have unlike denominators, find the least common multiple (LCM) and rename the fractions.

$\frac{1}{7} \bigcirc \frac{2}{3}$    The denominators are 3 and 7, so you must find the LCM of 3 and 7.

Multiples of 3: 3, 6, 9, 12, 15, 18, ㉑, 24
Multiples of 7: 7, 14, ㉑, 28

$\frac{1}{7} \times \frac{3}{3} = \frac{3}{21}$    The LCM of 3 and 7 is 21. Rename each fraction so that they both have the same denominator of 21.

$\frac{2}{3} \times \frac{7}{7} = \frac{14}{21}$    Multiply both the numerator and denominator by the same number.

$\frac{3}{21}$ < $\frac{14}{21}$    Look at the numerator to determine the larger fraction.

**Use >, <, or = to compare each pair of fractions.**

1. $\frac{4}{8} \bigcirc \frac{2}{10}$    2. $\frac{1}{5} \bigcirc \frac{2}{10}$    3. $\frac{3}{8} \bigcirc \frac{10}{12}$

4. $\frac{3}{12} \bigcirc \frac{1}{3}$    5. $\frac{2}{8} \bigcirc \frac{1}{4}$    6. $\frac{3}{6} \bigcirc \frac{4}{8}$

Spectrum Math Grade 4

Name _____

# Lesson 6.4 Adding Fractions with Like Denominators

To add fractions with like denominators, just add the numerators.

$\frac{2}{8} + \frac{5}{8}$

Write the sum over the common denominator.

$\frac{2}{8} + \frac{5}{8} = \frac{2+5}{8} = \frac{7}{8}$

**Add.**

1. $\frac{3}{12} + \frac{8}{12} =$ _____

2. $\frac{2}{5} + \frac{1}{5} =$ _____

3. $\frac{3}{6} + \frac{2}{6} =$ _____

4. $\frac{1}{10} + \frac{3}{10} =$ _____

5. $\frac{3}{8} + \frac{2}{8} =$ _____

6. $\frac{1}{3} + \frac{1}{3} =$ _____

7. $\frac{1}{4} + \frac{2}{4} =$ _____

8. $\frac{3}{5} + \frac{1}{5} =$ _____

9. $\frac{3}{10} + \frac{6}{10} =$ _____

10. $\frac{3}{8} + \frac{2}{8}$

11. $\frac{3}{12} + \frac{4}{12}$

12. $\frac{1}{6} + \frac{1}{6}$

13. $\frac{7}{10} + \frac{2}{10}$

14. $\frac{5}{11} + \frac{3}{11}$

15. $\frac{3}{7} + \frac{4}{7}$

16. $\frac{4}{9} + \frac{3}{9}$

17. $\frac{8}{9} + \frac{3}{9}$

Spectrum Math Grade 4

Name _____

# Lesson 6.5 Subtracting Fractions with Like Denominators

To subtract fractions with like denominators, just subtract the numerators.

$\frac{5}{8} - \frac{2}{8}$

Write the difference over the common denominator.

$\frac{5}{8} - \frac{2}{8} = \frac{5-2}{8} = \frac{3}{8}$

**Subtract.**

1. $\frac{11}{12} - \frac{3}{12}$
2. $\frac{7}{10} - \frac{3}{10}$
3. $\frac{3}{4} - \frac{1}{4}$
4. $\frac{6}{7} - \frac{5}{7}$

5. $\frac{5}{10} - \frac{3}{10}$
6. $\frac{8}{12} - \frac{7}{12}$
7. $\frac{4}{5} - \frac{2}{5}$
8. $\frac{7}{10} - \frac{4}{10}$

9. $\frac{5}{8} - \frac{1}{8}$
10. $\frac{9}{10} - \frac{3}{10}$
11. $\frac{8}{9} - \frac{1}{9}$
12. $\frac{8}{11} - \frac{5}{11}$

Name _____

# Lesson 6.6 Decomposing Fractions

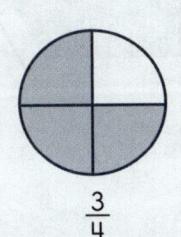

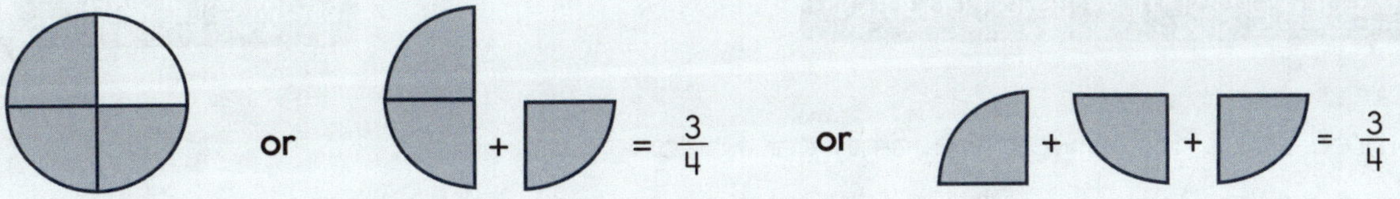

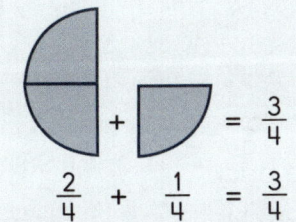

$\frac{3}{4}$  or  $\frac{2}{4} + \frac{1}{4} = \frac{3}{4}$  or  $\frac{1}{4} + \frac{1}{4} + \frac{1}{4} = \frac{3}{4}$

**Decompose each fraction in two ways. Write two equations to show your thinking.**

1. $\frac{3}{5}$

2. $\frac{5}{6}$

3. $\frac{4}{12}$

4. $\frac{3}{8}$

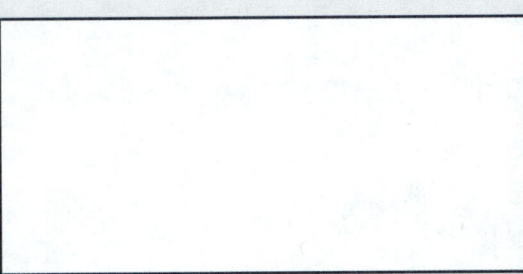

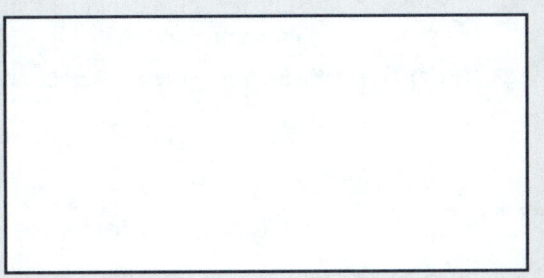

Spectrum Math Grade 4

107

Name _____

# Lesson 6.7 Problem Solving

**Solve each problem. Write an equation.**  **Show your work.**

1. Three sisters had to wash the family car. Paula washed the front $\frac{1}{3}$ and Kelley washed the back $\frac{1}{3}$ of the car. Mandy didn't show up to wash her part of the car. How much of the car was washed?

    _____ of the car was washed.

2. Autumn has a bag of apples to feed her horses. If she feeds $\frac{2}{4}$ of the bag to her favorite horse and $\frac{1}{4}$ to the new foal, how much of the bag is left to feed the other horses?

    _____ of a bag of apples is left for the other horses.

3. The library received $\frac{3}{5}$ of its book order one day. The next day, it received $\frac{1}{5}$ of the order. How much of the book order does the library have?

    The library has _____ of the book order.

4. A group of friends went to the movies. In the lobby, $\frac{4}{8}$ of the group decided to see a comedy and $\frac{2}{8}$ decided to see a mystery. How much of the group wanted to see either a comedy or a mystery?

    _____ of the group wanted to see a comedy or a mystery.

Spectrum Math Grade 4

Name _____

# Lesson 6.8 Understanding Decimals to Tenths

Decimals can be shown as fractions on a model or on a number line.

$0.4 = \frac{4}{10}$ = four-tenths = [model] = [number line with $\frac{4}{10}$ or 0.4 marked]

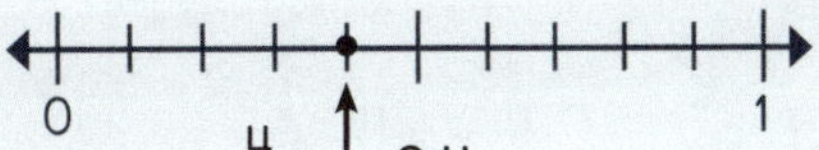

**Write the decimal and fraction for the shaded portion of each box.**

1. 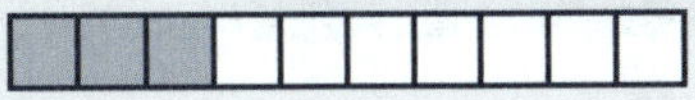 _____ or _____

2.  _____ or _____

3.  _____ or _____

**Write the decimal for each fraction.**

4. $\frac{2}{10}$ = _____

5. $\frac{6}{10}$ = _____

6. $\frac{9}{10}$ = _____

7. $\frac{4}{10}$ = _____

8. $\frac{3}{10}$ = _____

9. $\frac{1}{10}$ = _____

10. $\frac{8}{10}$ = _____

11. $\frac{5}{10}$ = _____

**Locate each on the number line. Draw a dot.**

12. $\frac{2}{10}$

13. 0.8

14. $\frac{6}{10}$

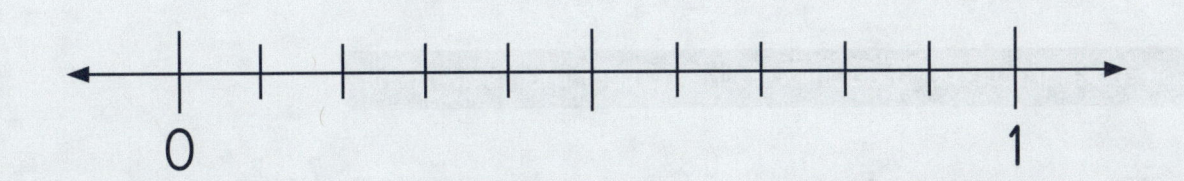

Spectrum Math Grade 4

# Lesson 6.9 Understanding Decimals to Hundredths

$0.34 = \frac{34}{100}$ = thirty-four hundredths =

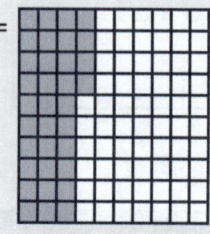

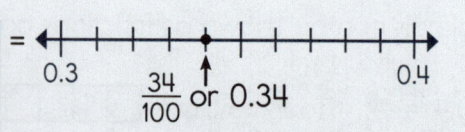

**Write the decimal and fraction for each shaded portion of the hundredths square.**

1. 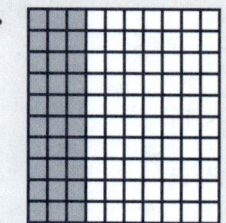 _____ or _____

2. 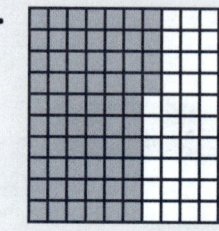 _____ or _____

3.  _____ or _____

4. 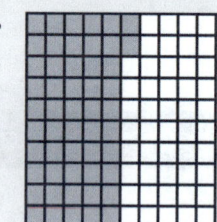 _____ or _____

**Locate each fraction and decimal on the number line. Draw a dot.**

5. $\frac{47}{100}$

6. 0.83

7. $\frac{2}{10}$

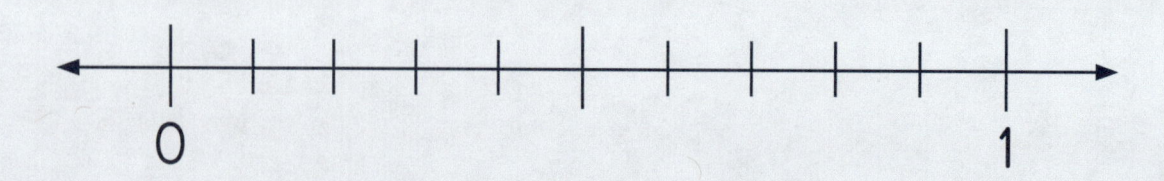

110

Spectrum Math Grade 4

Name _____

# Lesson 6.10 Adding Fractions with Unlike Denominators

To add fractions with unlike denominators, make the denominators the same.

$$\frac{1}{10} \qquad \frac{1}{10} = \frac{10}{100} \qquad \frac{10}{100}$$
$$+\frac{6}{100} \qquad\qquad\qquad\qquad +\frac{6}{100}$$
$$\qquad\qquad\qquad\qquad\qquad \overline{\frac{16}{100}}$$

**Add.**

1. $\frac{1}{10}$
   $+\frac{9}{100}$

2. $\frac{2}{10}$
   $+\frac{2}{100}$

3. $\frac{4}{10}$
   $+\frac{5}{100}$

4. $\frac{7}{10}$
   $+\frac{7}{100}$

5. $\frac{4}{10}$
   $+\frac{8}{100}$

6. $\frac{6}{10}$
   $+\frac{5}{100}$

7. $\frac{5}{10}$
   $+\frac{2}{100}$

8. $\frac{3}{10}$
   $+\frac{6}{100}$

9. $\frac{8}{10}$
   $+\frac{3}{100}$

Spectrum Math Grade 4

# Lesson 6.11 Adding Mixed Numbers with Like Denominators

$3\frac{4}{9}$
$+ 2\frac{2}{9}$

$\frac{4}{9} + \frac{2}{9} = \frac{6}{9}$   To add mixed numbers with like, or common, denominators, add the fractions.

$3 + 2 = 5$   Then, add the whole numbers.

$5\frac{6}{9} = 5\frac{2}{3}$   Reduce to simplest form. (Both 6 and 9 can be divided by 3.)

**Add. Write answers in simplest form.**

1. $3\frac{4}{7}$
   $+ 5\frac{3}{7}$

2. $6\frac{4}{9}$
   $+ 8\frac{5}{9}$

3. $7\frac{1}{6}$
   $+ 3\frac{1}{6}$

4. $2\frac{2}{5}$
   $+ 4\frac{4}{5}$

5. $3\frac{2}{11}$
   $+ 8\frac{8}{11}$

6. $9\frac{3}{10}$
   $+ 2\frac{9}{10}$

7. $5\frac{1}{8}$
   $+ 4\frac{3}{8}$

8. $1\frac{6}{7}$
   $+ 3\frac{2}{7}$

9. $8\frac{3}{4}$
   $+ 6\frac{3}{4}$

# Lesson 6.12 Subtracting Mixed Numbers with Like Denominators

$3\frac{1}{10}$
$-1\frac{3}{10}$

$\overset{2}{\cancel{3}}\overset{11}{\cancel{\frac{1}{10}}} - 1\frac{3}{10}$   $\frac{1}{10}$ is less than $\frac{3}{10}$. Regroup and rename $3\frac{1}{10}$ as $2\frac{11}{10}$.

$\frac{11}{10} - \frac{3}{10} = \frac{8}{10}$   Subtract the fractions.

$2 - 1 = 1$   Subtract the whole numbers.

$1\frac{8}{10} = 1\frac{4}{5}$   Put them together. Then simplify if needed.

**Subtract. Write answers in simplest form.**

1. $3\frac{3}{4}$
   $-1\frac{1}{4}$

2. $6\frac{2}{7}$
   $-2\frac{1}{7}$

3. $9\frac{7}{8}$
   $-3\frac{5}{8}$

4. $6\frac{3}{8}$
   $-3\frac{6}{8}$

5. $7\frac{7}{9}$
   $-4\frac{4}{9}$

6. $5\frac{7}{10}$
   $-3\frac{1}{10}$

7. $6\frac{3}{5}$
   $-4\frac{2}{5}$

8. $9\frac{3}{7}$
   $-7\frac{3}{7}$

9. $8\frac{7}{9}$
   $-7\frac{2}{9}$

Spectrum Math Grade 4

**Name** _____

## Lesson 6.13 Problem Solving

**Solve each problem.**  **Show your work.**

1. It takes Carlos $2\frac{1}{6}$ days to make a model airplane and $1\frac{5}{6}$ days to make a model car. How many days will it take Carlos to make both?

   It will take _____ days for Carlos to make both.

2. Mr. Chen is going to the post office with two packages. One package weighs $6\frac{3}{8}$ kilograms and the other weighs $2\frac{1}{8}$ kilograms. How many kilograms are the two packages combined?

   The packages weigh _____ kilograms combined.

3. The beach is $6\frac{9}{10}$ miles from the Cabrera family. They have driven $2\frac{3}{10}$ miles toward the beach. How many more miles must the Cabrera family drive?

   The Cabrera family must drive _____ more miles.

4. Leila wants to paint her bedroom blue and gold. She has $4\frac{3}{8}$ gallons of blue paint and $2\frac{1}{8}$ gallons of gold paint. How much more blue paint does Leila have than gold paint?

   Leila has _____ more gallons of blue paint than gold paint.

Spectrum Math Grade 4

# Lesson 6.14 Fractions as Multiples

Just like we use repeated addition to understand multiplication, we can decompose fractions into smaller but equal parts. Then, we can multiply.

$$\frac{4}{5} = \frac{1}{5} + \frac{1}{5} + \frac{1}{5} + \frac{1}{5} \qquad \frac{4}{5} = 4 \times \left(\frac{1}{5}\right)$$

**Write the multiplication equation and addition equation for each fraction.**

1. $\frac{7}{3} =$

   ___ × (———)

   or

   _____

2. $\frac{2}{8} =$

   ___ × (———)

   or

   _____

3. $\frac{6}{10} =$

   ___ × (———)

   or

   _____

4. $\frac{2}{4} =$

   ___ × (———)

   or

   _____

5. $\frac{10}{6} =$

   ___ × (———)

   or

   _____

6. $\frac{5}{12} =$

   ___ × (———)

   or

   _____

Spectrum Math Grade 4

Name _____

# Lesson 6.15 Multiplying Fractions and Whole Numbers

To multiply fractions and whole numbers, follow these steps.

$\frac{2}{3} \times 6 = \frac{2}{3} \times \frac{6}{1}$   Rewrite the whole number as a fraction.

$\frac{2 \times 6}{3 \times 1} = \frac{12}{3}$   Multiply the numerators. Multiply the denominators.

$\frac{12}{3} = 4$   Reduce to simplest form.

**Multiply. Write answers in simplest form.**

1. $3 \times \frac{1}{8} =$ _____

2. $5 \times \frac{2}{3} =$ _____

3. $\frac{2}{9} \times 8 =$ _____

4. $\frac{4}{7} \times 2 =$ _____

5. $6 \times \frac{3}{5} =$ _____

6. $2 \times \frac{5}{9} =$ _____

7. $\frac{2}{7} \times 3 =$ _____

8. $7 \times \frac{3}{4} =$ _____

9. $\frac{8}{9} \times 4 =$ _____

10. $\frac{1}{2} \times 8 =$ _____

11. $\frac{4}{5} \times 6 =$ _____

12. $9 \times \frac{1}{3} =$ _____

Name _____

## Lesson 6.16 Problem Solving

**Solve each problem.**  **Show your work.**

1. One serving of pancakes calls for $\frac{1}{3}$ cup of milk. How many cups of milk are needed for 4 servings of pancakes?

   _____ cups of milk are needed.

2. Tony had 2 gallons of orange juice. This week, he drank $\frac{4}{7}$ of the orange juice he had. How much orange juice did Tony drink?

   He drank _____ gallons of orange juice.

3. A single serving of gelatin dessert requires $\frac{3}{8}$ cup sugar. How much sugar is needed for 6 servings?

   _____ cups of sugar are needed.

4. Jason put down tiles on his basement floor. He placed 10 tiles in the first row. Each square tile is $\frac{5}{8}$ feet in length. How long is the first row of tiles?

   The first row of tiles is _____ feet long.

Spectrum Math Grade 4

117

Name _____

**Posttest** Chapter 6

Find the equivalent fraction.

1. $\frac{3}{5} = \frac{\phantom{0}}{25}$
2. $\frac{2}{6} = \frac{\phantom{0}}{18}$
3. $\frac{1}{2} = \frac{9}{\phantom{0}}$
4. $\frac{2}{8} = \frac{10}{\phantom{0}}$

Compare the fractions using >, <, or =.

5. $\frac{1}{2} \bigcirc \frac{2}{10}$
6. $\frac{1}{2} \bigcirc \frac{3}{4}$
7. $\frac{7}{10} \bigcirc \frac{3}{5}$
8. $\frac{3}{8} \bigcirc \frac{2}{6}$

Add or subtract.

9. $\frac{1}{4} + \frac{1}{4}$
10. $\frac{8}{9} - \frac{1}{9}$
11. $\frac{5}{12} + \frac{3}{12}$
12. $\frac{5}{10} - \frac{3}{10}$

Decompose each fraction.

13. $\frac{3}{5}$
14. $\frac{7}{8}$
15. $\frac{2}{6}$
16. $\frac{5}{7}$

Write the decimal equivalent for each given fraction.

17. $\frac{8}{100} = $ _____
18. $\frac{4}{10} = $ _____
19. $\frac{45}{100} = $ _____

118

Spectrum Math Grade 4

# Posttest Chapter 6

**Add or subtract. Write answers in simplest form.**

20. $\frac{6}{10} + \frac{5}{100}$

21. $6\frac{1}{7} - 2\frac{5}{7}$

22. $6\frac{4}{11} + 1\frac{3}{11}$

23. $\frac{3}{10} + \frac{3}{100}$

24. $7\frac{7}{9} - 4\frac{4}{9}$

25. $6\frac{3}{5} - 5\frac{1}{5}$

26. $6\frac{8}{9} - 3\frac{7}{9}$

27. $3\frac{4}{7} + 5\frac{3}{7}$

**Multiply. Write answers in simplest form.**

28. $8 \times \frac{8}{9} =$ _____

29. $\frac{5}{12} \times 6 =$ _____

30. $\frac{3}{8} \times 3 =$ _____

31. $7 \times \frac{4}{11} =$ _____

32. $\frac{1}{4} \times 3 =$ _____

33. $\frac{1}{2} \times 9 =$ _____

34. $\frac{3}{5} \times 2 =$ _____

35. $4 \times \frac{7}{10} =$ _____

36. $\frac{2}{3} \times 8 =$ _____

Spectrum Math Grade 4

# Chapter 7: Measurement

## Helpful Definitions

**US customary units:** units of measurement used in the United States

**metric units:** units of measurement based on the meter and gram

**perimeter:** the distance around a shape; for example, add the lengths of all of the sides to find the perimeter: 12 cm + 7 cm + 12 cm + 7 cm = 38 cm

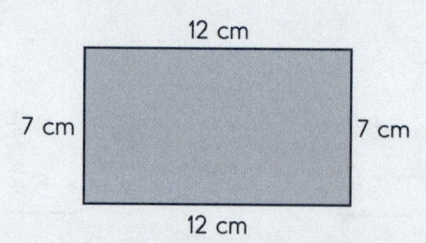

**area:** the amount of space a shape covers; for example, multiply the length by the width: 15 inches × 3 inches = 45 square inches

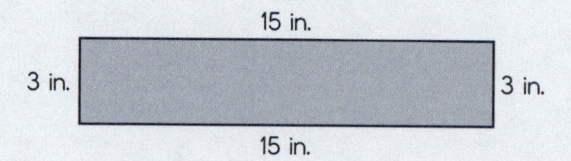

**angles:** created by the joining of rays or intersecting lines, it is the measure of the space between the rays

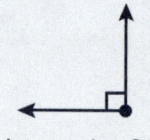

right angle: 90°

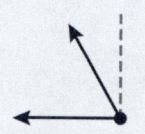

acute angle: (measures less than 90°)

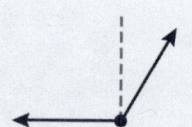

obtuse angle: (measures more than 90°, but less than 180°)

## Skills Checklist

☐ Use customary units to measure length, capacity, and weight

☐ Use metric units to measure length, capacity, and weight

☐ Solve word problems using measurements

☐ Measure perimeter and area

☐ Solve word problems using perimeter and area

☐ Create line plots with measurement data

☐ Measure, name, and draw angles

## Tools and Tips

There are lots of ways to measure different items. People measure the length of an object, such as a rug or a skateboard. We measure the volume of liquids, such as water, or the weight of objects, such as a bag of flour. Your student may measure a variety of items that are important to their daily lives, such as their own weight.

Help your student measure a variety of items in both standard and metric measurements. For example, have them measure how much water they drink in a day in ounces and in liters. If they drink about 64 ounces of water, that is about 2 liters. Using both types of measurements for the same item will help your student understand customary and metric units.

### US Customary Unit Conversions

| Length | Weight | Capacity |
|---|---|---|
| 12 inches (in.) = 1 foot (ft.) | $\frac{1}{2}$ pound (lb.) = 8 ounces (oz.) | 1 cup (c.) = 8 ounces (oz.) |
| 3 feet = 1 yard (yd.) | 1 pound = 16 ounces | 1 pint (pt.) = 2 cups |
| 36 inches = 1 yard | $\frac{1}{2}$ ton (T.) = 1,000 pounds | 1 quart (qt.) = 2 pints |
| 1,760 yards = 1 mile (mi.) | 1 ton = 2,000 pounds | 1 gallon (gal.) = 4 quarts |
| 5,280 feet = 1 mile |  | 1 gallon = 8 pints |
|  |  | 1 gallon = 16 cups |

### Metric Unit Conversions

| Length | Weight | Capacity |
|---|---|---|
| 1 kilometer (km) = 1,000 meters (m) | 1 kilogram (kg) = 1,000 grams (g) | 1 kiloliter (kL) = 1,000 liters (L) |
| 1 meter = 0.001 kilometers | 1 gram = 0.001 kilograms | 1 liter = 0.001 kiloliters |
| 1 meter = 100 centimeters (cm) | 1 gram = 100 centigrams (cg) | 1 liter = 100 centiliters (cL) |
| 1 centimeter = 0.01 meters | 1 centigram = 0.01 grams | 1 centiliter = 0.01 liters |
| 1 meter = 1,000 millimeters (mm) | 1 gram = 1,000 milligrams (mg) | 1 liter = 1,000 milliliters (mL) |
| 1 centimeter = 10 millimeters | 1 milligram = 0.001 grams | 1 milliliter = 0.001 liters |

Name _____

**Pretest** Chapter 7

Complete the following conversions.

1. 36 inches = _____ yard
2. 8 quarts = _____ gallons
3. 1 cup = _____ ounces

4. 1 mile = _____ yards
5. 2 feet = _____ inches
6. 10 cups = _____ pints

7. 3 feet = _____ yard
8. 8 pints = _____ quarts
9. 10 pints = _____ cups

Find the area and perimeter of each shape.

10. 10 yd. / 30 yd.

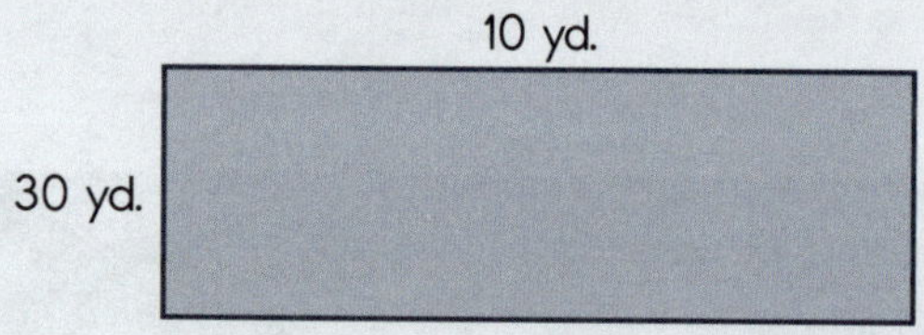

P = _____ yards

A = _____ square yards

11. 12 in. / 6 in.

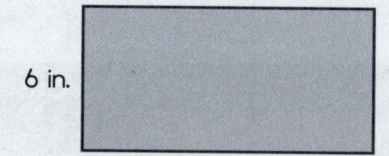

P = _____ inches

A = _____ square inches

Measure each angle.

12.

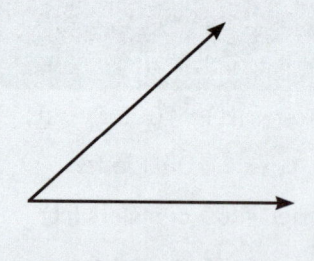

_____ °

13.

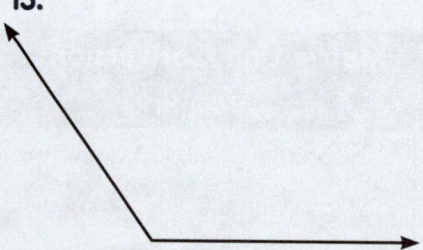

_____ °

14.

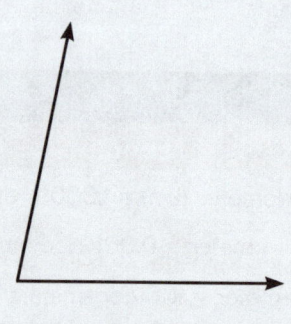

_____ °

122

Spectrum Math Grade 4

Name _____

**Pretest** Chapter 7

Solve each problem.   Show your work.

15. Paul is using a 4-quart container to fill a wash tub. If he needs 12 gallons of water to fill the tub, how many times does he need to fill the 4-quart container?

    He needs to fill the container _____ times.

16. A worker at the zoo measured the length of an iguana. The iguana measured 72 inches long. How many feet did the iguana measure?

    The iguana measured _____ feet.

17. The feed store has a half ton of wood shavings to ship to the horse farm. How many pounds of shavings does the feed store have?

    The feed store has _____ pounds of wood shavings.

18. The city of Concord is planning a skateboard park and needs to know the perimeter of the park. The edges of the property measure 7 yards, 3 yards, 10 yards, and 5 yards. What is the perimeter?

    The property's perimeter is _____ yards.

Spectrum Math Grade 4

Name _____

**Pretest** Chapter 7

**Complete the following conversions.**

**19.** 5 km = _____ m     **20.** 60,000 mL = _____ L     **21.** 6 m = _____ cm

**22.** 32 kg = _____ g     **23.** 72 cm = _____ mm     **24.** 19 L = _____ mL

**25.** 1 g = _____ mg     **26.** 100 cm = _____ m     **27.** 25 kg = _____ g

**28.** 200 mm = _____ cm     **29.** 17 L = _____ mL     **30.** 5,200 cm = _____ m

**Use the line plot to answer the questions.**

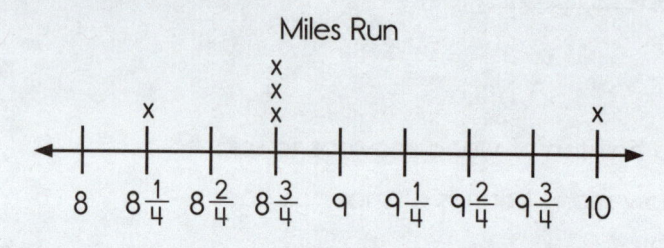

Miles Run

**31.** What is the difference between the longest distance run and the shortest distance run?

_____

**32.** If you add all of the distances together, what would be the total distance run?

_____

**Find each missing angle.**

**33.** ? 18°  _____°

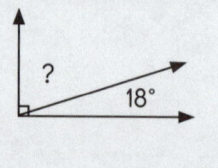

**34.** ? 73°  _____°

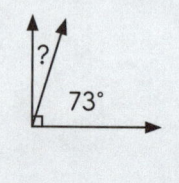

**35.** ? 81°  _____°

124

Spectrum Math Grade 4

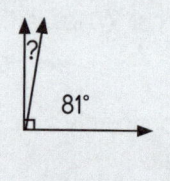

Name _____

**Pretest** Chapter 7

**Solve each problem.**        Show your work.

36. A hiking trail is 35 kilometers long. Sarah hiked 15 kilometers so far. How many more meters does Sarah have to hike?

    Sarah has to hike _____ more meters.

37. The ham in the store weighs 1 kilogram, the turkey weighs 2 kilograms, and the chicken weighs 1 kilogram. How many grams do all three items in the grocery store weigh?

    All three items weigh _____ grams.

38. Shawna needs liters of ginger ale and cola for a party, but the soda can only be ordered by the milliliter. If she orders 30,000 milliliters of ginger ale and 20,000 milliliters of cola, how many liters of soda will she have?

    She will have _____ liters of soda.

39. A science experiment requires students to measure 52,000 milligrams of chemicals. There are only 13,000 milligrams of chemicals in the science lab. How many more milligrams of chemicals do the students need?

    The students need _____ more milligrams of chemicals.

Spectrum Math Grade 4

Name _____

## Lesson 7.1 Customary Units of Length

| 12 inches (in.) = 1 foot (ft.) |
| 3 feet = 1 yard (yd.) |
| 36 inches = 1 yard |
| 1,760 yards = 1 mile (mi.) |
| 5,280 feet = 1 mile |

6 feet = ____ inches
(6 × 12 = 72)
6 feet = 72 inches

Think: How many inches in 1 foot? (12 inches)
To convert from a larger unit to a smaller unit, multiply.

84 feet = ____ yards
(84 ÷ 3 = 28)
84 feet = 28 yards

Think: How many feet in 1 yard? (3 feet)
To convert from a smaller unit to a larger unit, divide.

**Complete the following conversions.**

1. 5 yd. = _____ ft.
2. 8 ft. = _____ in.
3. 72 yd. = _____ ft.

4. 48 in. = _____ ft.
5. 3 mi. = _____ yd.
6. 24 yd. = _____ in.

7. 3,000 ft. = _____ yd.
8. 24 in. = _____ ft.
9. 2 mi. = _____ ft.

10. 12 in. = _____ ft.
11. 26 yd. = _____ in.
12. 12 ft. = _____ yd.

13. 360 in. = _____ yd.
14. 10 ft. = _____ in.
15. 720 yd. = _____ ft.

16. 7 mi. = _____ yd.
17. 2,400 in. = _____ ft.
18. 324 ft. = _____ yd.

Spectrum Math Grade 4

Name _____

# Lesson 7.2 Problem Solving

**Solve each problem.**  **Show your work.**

1. Brandy's playset has a curvy slide that is 5 feet long. Pedro's has a curvy slide that is 8 feet long. How many inches longer is Pedro's slide than Brandy's slide?

   Pedro's slide is _____ inches longer.

2. Kristi and Brian were competing in the long jump. Kristi jumped 9 feet. Brian jumped 6 feet. How many total yards did Kristi and Brian jump together?

   They jumped a total of _____ yards.

3. The new speedboat measures 25 yards long. The old speedboat measured 18 yards long. How many feet longer is the new speedboat than the old speedboat?

   The new speedboat is _____ feet longer.

4. A brown snake measures 12 feet long. A green snake measures 15 feet long. How many yards long are both the brown snake and the green snake?

   Both snakes together are _____ yards long.

Spectrum Math Grade 4

127

## Lesson 7.3 Customary Units of Capacity

| |
|---|
| 1 cup = 8 ounces (oz.) |
| 1 pint = 2 cups (c.) |
| 1 quart = 2 pints (pt.) |
| 1 quart = 4 cups |
| 1 gallon = 4 quarts (qt.) |
| 1 gallon = 8 pints |
| 1 gallon = 16 cups |

7 quarts = ____ pints
(7 × 2 = 14)
7 quarts = 14 pints

16 quarts = ____ gallons
(16 ÷ 4 = 4)
16 quarts = 4 gallons

Think: How many pints in 1 quart?
(2 pints)
To convert from a larger unit to a smaller unit, multiply.

Think: How many quarts in 1 gallon?
(4 quarts)
To convert from a smaller unit to a larger unit, divide.

**Complete the following conversions.**

1. 2 gal. = _____ qt.
2. 4 pt. = _____ qt.
3. 12 c. = _____ pt.

4. 24 qt. = _____ gal.
5. 16 oz. = _____ c.
6. 10 qt. = _____ pt.

7. 14 pt. = _____ qt.
8. 28 qt. = _____ gal.
9. 14 pt. = _____ c.

10. 48 c. = _____ pt.
11. 32 oz. = _____ c.
12. 14 c. = _____ pt.

13. 10 gal. = _____ qt.
14. 30 pt. = _____ c.
15. 18 c. = _____ pt.

16. 12 gal. = _____ qt.
17. 22 pt. = _____ qt.
18. 64 oz. = _____ c.

**Name** _____

# Lesson 7.4 Customary Units of Weight

| $\frac{1}{2}$ pound (lb.) = 8 ounces |
|---|
| 1 pound = 16 ounces |
| $\frac{1}{2}$ ton (T.) = 1,000 pounds |
| 1 ton = 2,000 pounds |

5 pounds = ___ ounces
(5 × 16 = 80)
5 pounds = 80 ounces

6,000 pounds = ___ tons
(6,000 ÷ 2,000 = 3)
6,000 pounds = 3 tons

Think: How many ounces in 1 pound? (16 ounces)
To convert from a larger unit to a smaller unit, multiply.

Think: How many pounds in 1 ton? (2,000 pounds)
To convert from a smaller unit to a larger unit, divide.

**Complete the following conversions.**

1. 32 oz. = _____ lb.
2. 6,000 lb. = _____ T.
3. 4 T. = _____ lb.

4. 40 lb. = _____ oz.
5. 64 oz. = _____ lb.
6. 24,000 lb. = _____ T.

7. 1,000 lb. = _____ T.
8. 8 oz. = _____ lb.
9. 18,000 lb. = _____ T.

10. 8 lb. = _____ oz.
11. 12 lb. = _____ oz.
12. 10,000 lb. = _____ T.

**Write the missing equivalent weights.**

| | Tons | Pounds | Ounces |
|---|---|---|---|
| 13. | 5 | _____ | 160,000 |
| 14. | _____ | 4,000 | 64,000 |
| 15. | 3 | 6,000 | _____ |
| 16. | _____ | 2,000 | 32,000 |

Spectrum Math Grade 4

129

Name _____

## Lesson 7.5 Problem Solving

**Solve each problem.**  **Show your work.**

1. The cooks made 120 quarts of lemonade for the first concert. They made 150 quarts of lemonade for the second concert and 130 quarts for the third concert. How many gallons of lemonade did the cooks make for all three concerts?

   They made _____ gallons of lemonade in all.

2. A large ship was being loaded with 20 tons of grain and 5 tons of flour. How many more pounds of grain were there on the ship?

   There were _____ more pounds of grain.

3. The largest wheel of cheese in City A weighs 985 pounds. The largest wheel of cheese in City B weighs 894 pounds. How many total ounces do both wheels of cheese weigh?

   They weigh a total of _____ ounces.

4. Tito stored 15 gallons of water in his basement. Jack stored 29 gallons of water in his basement. During the hurricane, they used 32 gallons of water. How many quarts of water did the boys have left after the hurricane?

   Tito and Jack had _____ quarts of water left.

Spectrum Math Grade 4

Name _____

## Lesson 7.6 Metric Units of Length

Metric units of length are more easily converted than customary units of length. Understand the base ten number needed and you can convert easily between units.

| 10 millimeters (mm) = 1 centimeter (cm) |
| 100 centimeters = 1 meter (m) |
| 1,000 meters = 1 kilometer (km) |

7 cm = ____ mm
(7 × 10 = 70)
7 cm = 70 mm

Think: How many millimeters in 1 centimeter? (10)
To convert from a larger unit to a smaller unit, multiply.

3,000 mm = ____ m
(3,000 ÷ 1,000 = 3)
3,000 mm = 3 m

Think: How many millimeters in 1 meter? (1,000)
To convert from a smaller unit to a larger unit, divide.

**Complete the following conversions.**

1. 4 m = _____ cm
2. 25 m = _____ mm
3. 21 km = _____ m

4. 25 cm = _____ mm
5. 33 m = _____ cm
6. 14 km = _____ m

7. 15 m = _____ cm
8. 47 m = _____ mm
9. 5 km = _____ m

10. 84 cm = _____ mm
11. 75 m = _____ cm
12. 2 m = _____ cm

13. 10 km = _____ m
14. 66 m = _____ mm
15. 21 cm = _____ mm

Spectrum Math Grade 4

Name _____

## Lesson 7.7 Metric Units of Capacity

| 1 liter (l) = 1,000 milliliters (mL) |
| 1,000 liters = 1 kiloliter (kL) |

4 liters = ____ milliliters
(4 × 1,000 = 4,000)
4 liters = 4,000 milliliters

Think: How many milliliters in 1 liter? (1,000)
To convert from a larger unit to a smaller unit, multiply.

2,000 liters = ____ kiloliters
(2,000 ÷ 1,000 = 2)
2,000 liters = 2 kiloliters

Think: How many milliliters in 1 liter? (1,000)
To convert from a larger unit to a smaller unit, multiply.

**Complete the following conversions.**

1. 3 L = _____ mL      2. 12 L = _____ mL      3. 2 L = _____ mL

4. 75 L = _____ mL     5. 10 L = _____ mL      6. 50 L = _____ mL

7. 13 L = _____ mL     8. 78 L = _____ mL      9. 8 L = _____ mL

10. 9,000 mL = _____ L   11. 7,000 mL = _____ L   12. 2,000 mL = _____ L

132

Spectrum Math Grade 4

Name _____

# Lesson 7.8 Metric Units of Weight

| 1 gram (g) = 1,000 milligrams (mg) |
| 1,000 grams = 1 kilogram (kg) |

13 g = ___ mg
(13 × 1,000 = 13,000)
13 g = 13,000 mg

Think: How many milligrams in 1 gram? (1,000)
To convert from a larger unit to a smaller unit, multiply.

5,000 g = ___ kg
(5,000 ÷ 1,000 = 5)
5,000 g = 5 kg

Think: How many grams in 1 kilogram? (1,000)
To convert from a smaller unit to a larger unit, divide.

**Complete the following conversions.**

1. 16 kg = _____ g

2. 32 g = _____ mg

3. 45 kg = _____ g

4. 10 g = _____ mg

5. 42 kg = _____ g

6. 9 g = _____ mg

7. 105 g = _____ mg

8. 37 g = _____ mg

9. 12 kg = _____ g

10. 183 kg = _____ g

11. 18 g = _____ mg

12. 119 kg = _____ g

13. 9,000 mg = _____ g

14. 45 kg = _____ g

15. 6,000 mg = _____ g

Spectrum Math Grade 4

Name _____

## Lesson 7.9 Problem Solving

**Solve each problem.**   **Show your work.**

1. Ben pours 500 milliliters of milk from a full 1-liter bottle into his cereal. How much is left in the bottle?

   _____ milliliters are left in the bottle.

2. The bakery needs 15 pounds of flour. They buy their flour in 50-ounce bags. How many bags should they buy?

   The bakery should buy _____ bags of flour.

3. Mr. Ortega bought 2 pounds 4 ounces of ground beef for an upcoming backyard barbecue. He freezes 20 ounces and makes patties out of the rest. How many ounces of ground beef does he cook?

   He cooks _____ ounces of ground beef.

4. Ms. Mayberry has a 2-liter jug of juice. She is pouring it into 200-milliliter cups. How many cups will she fill?

   Ms. Mayberry will fill _____ cups.

Name ______________________________

## **Lesson 7.10** Measuring Perimeter

**Perimeter** is the distance around a shape. To find the perimeter, add together the lengths of all the sides.

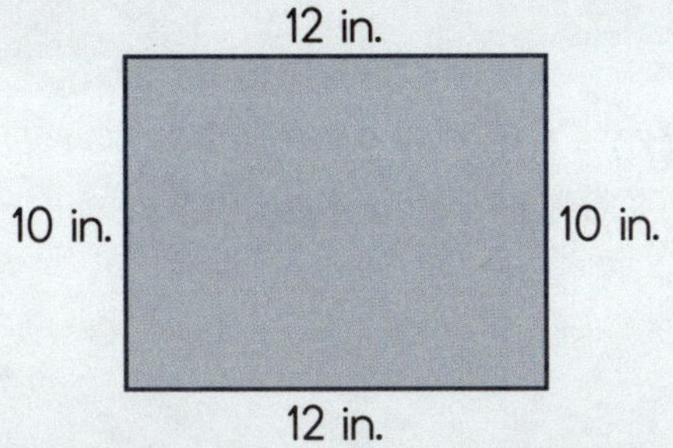
12 in.
10 in.
10 in.
12 in.

Perimeter ($P$) = 12 in. + 10 in. + 12 in. + 10 in.
$P$ = 44 in.

**Find the perimeter of each shape.**

**1.**

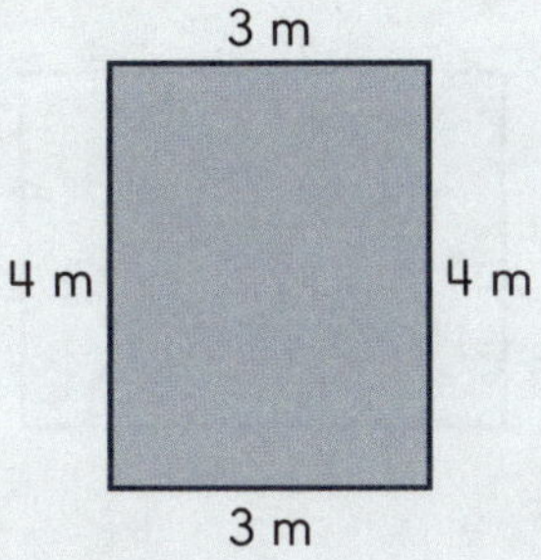
3 m
4 m
4 m
3 m

________ m

**2.**

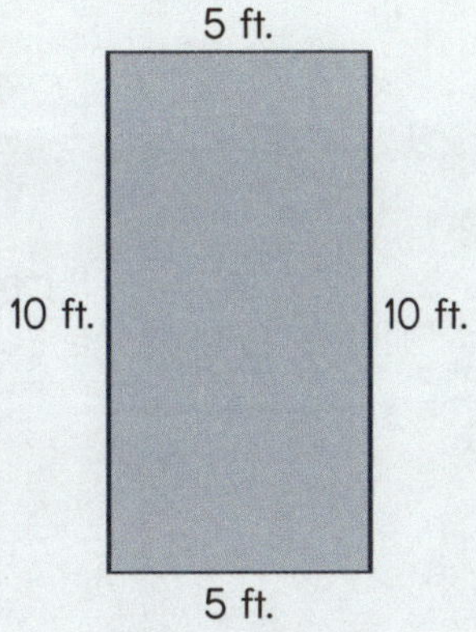
5 ft.
10 ft.
10 ft.
5 ft.

________ ft.

**3.**

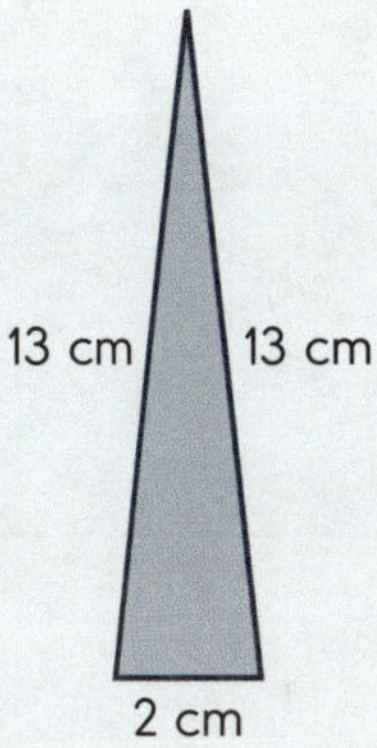
13 cm
13 cm
2 cm

________ cm

**4.**

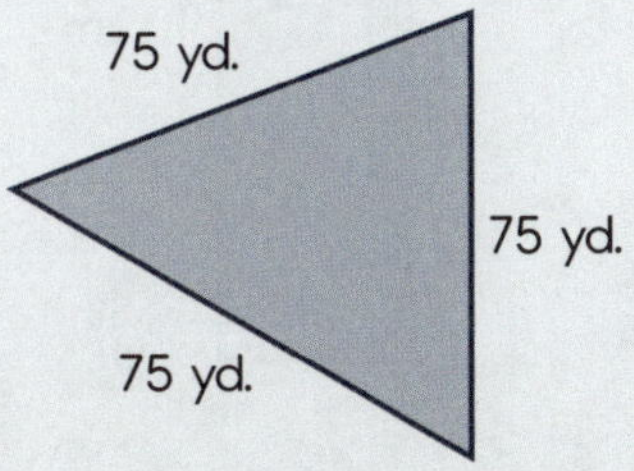
75 yd.
75 yd.
75 yd.

________ yd.

**5.**

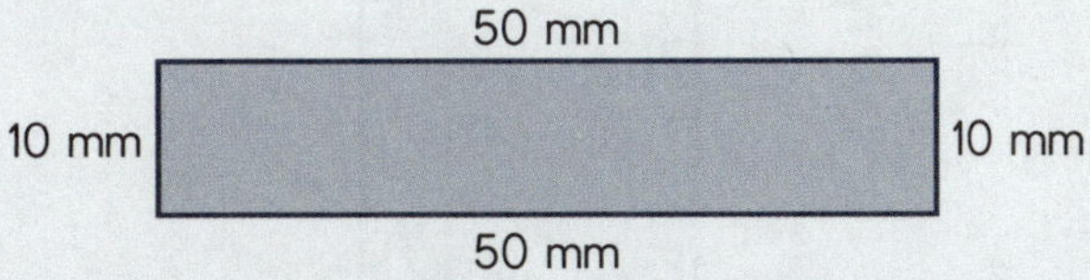
50 mm
10 mm
10 mm
50 mm

________ mm

**6.**

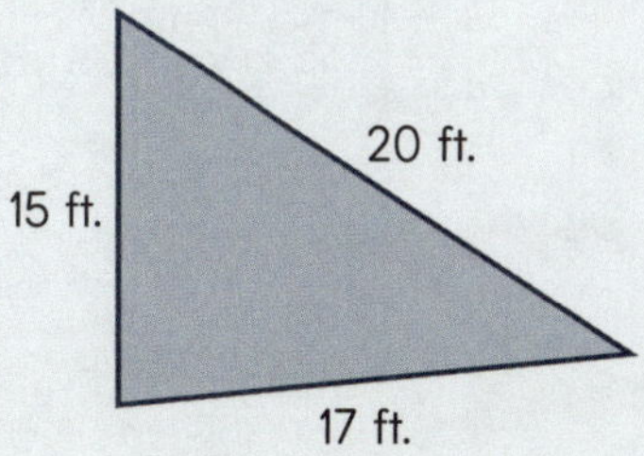
20 ft.
15 ft.
17 ft.

________ ft.

Name _____

## Lesson 7.11 Measuring Area

**Area** is the amount of space a shape covers. To find the area of a square or rectangle, multiply length by width.

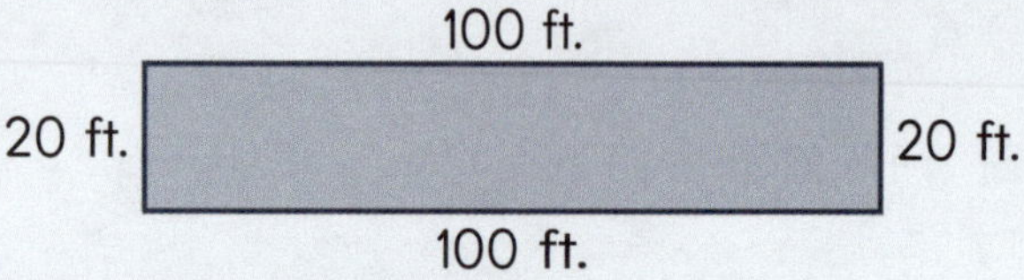

Area (A) = 100 ft. × 20 ft.
A = 2,000 square feet (sq. ft.)

**Find the area of each shape.**

1.
15 in.
13 in.

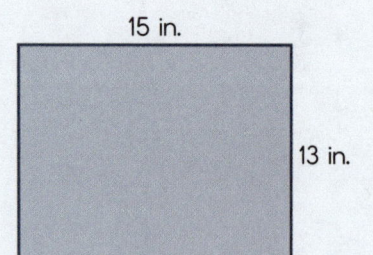

_____ sq. in.

2.
11 mm
11 mm

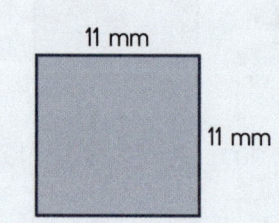

_____ sq. mm

3.
12 ft.
11 ft.

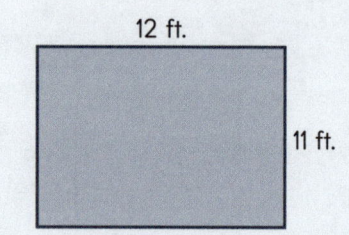

_____ sq. ft.

4.
10 yd.
25 yd.

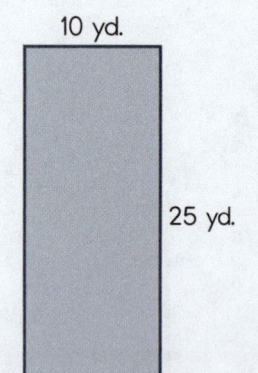

_____ sq. yd.

5.
5 cm
8 cm

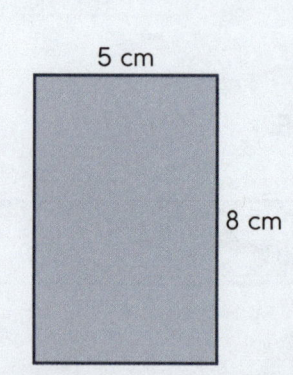

_____ sq. cm

6.
12 km
40 km

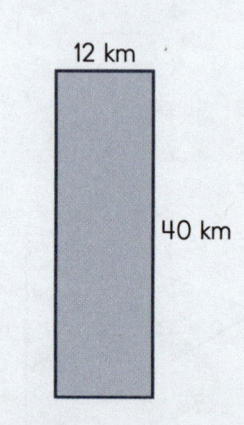

_____ sq. km

Name _____

# Lesson 7.12 Problem Solving

**Solve each problem.**  **Show your work.**

1. John cleared a vacant lot to plant a garden. The lot measured 35 feet by 15 feet. What is the perimeter of the garden lot?

   The perimeter of the lot is _____ feet.

2. Freda is putting carpet down in a room that measures 20 feet long by 30 feet wide. What is the area of the room?

   The area is _____ square feet.

3. The zoo is building a new hippo pool that will measure 55 feet by 75 feet. What is the area of the pool?

   The area is _____ square feet.

4. Gabriel built a pen for his pet guinea pigs. The pen measures 14 feet by 12 feet. What is the perimeter of the pen?

   The perimeter of the pen is _____ feet.

Spectrum Math Grade 4

137

Name _____

## Lesson 7.13 Line Plots in Measurement

A **line plot** is a graph that displays data as Xs above a number line. It shows the frequency of each value.

| Length of Books on a Shelf in Inches | |
|---|---|
| 5 | IIII |
| $5\frac{1}{2}$ | III |
| 6 | II |
| $6\frac{1}{2}$ | IIII |
| 7 | IIII |

Length of Books on a Shelf in Inches

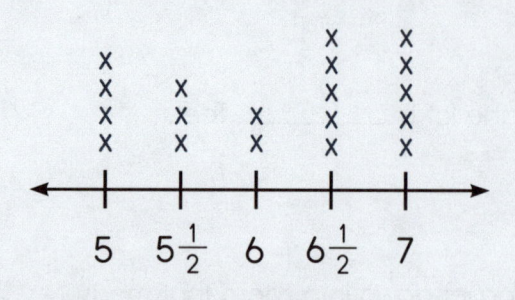

```
                    x    x
          x         x    x
x         x         x    x
x    x    x         x    x
x    x    x    x    x    x
←——+————+————+————+————+——→
   5   5½    6   6½    7
```

**Use the table to complete the line plot. Answer the questions.**

| Cups of Sugar Used in Cookie Recipes | |
|---|---|
| $4\frac{1}{2}$ | IIII |
| 5 | III |
| $5\frac{1}{2}$ | IIII |
| 6 | II |
| $6\frac{1}{2}$ | I |

Cups of Sugar Used in Cookie Recipes

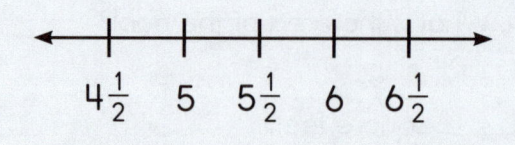

```
←——+————+————+————+————+——→
  4½   5   5½    6   6½
```

1. How many total cups of sugar were used to make cookies? _____

2. How many recipes used $5\frac{1}{2}$ cups of sugar? _____

3. What is the difference between the largest amount of sugar and the smallest amount of sugar? _____

138

Spectrum Math Grade 4

Name _____

## Lesson 7.14 Identifying Angles

A **right angle** measures exactly 90°.

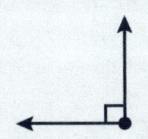

An **acute angle** measures less than 90°.

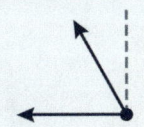

An **obtuse angle** measures greater than 90° but less than 180°.

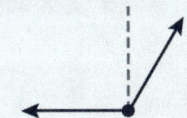

**Identify each angle as *right*, *acute*, or *obtuse*.**

1.

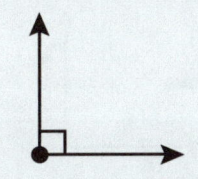

_____

2.

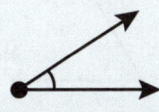

_____

3.

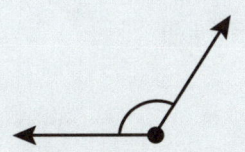

_____

4.

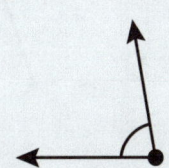

_____

5.

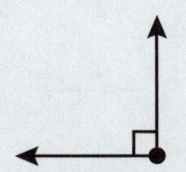

_____

6.

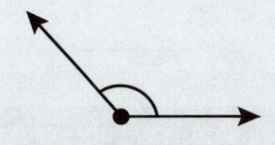

_____

Spectrum Math Grade 4

139

Name _____

## Lesson 7.15 Measuring and Drawing Angles

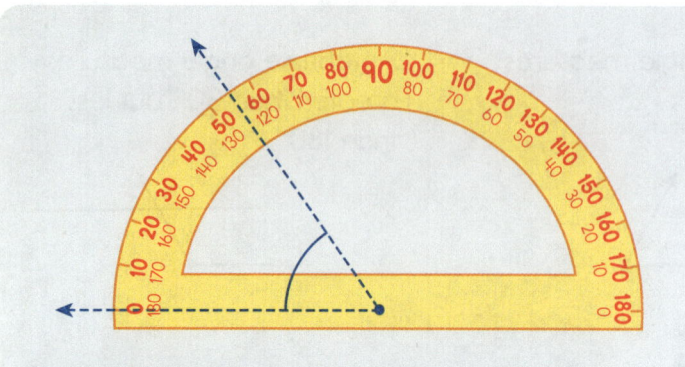

A **protractor** is used to measure an angle. The angle is measured in degrees.

Use a protractor to measure each angle.

1.

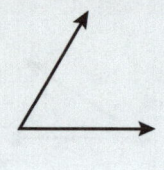

_____ °

2.

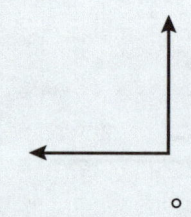

_____ °

3.

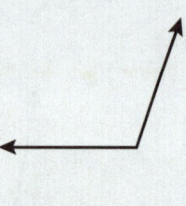

_____ °

4.

_____ °

5.

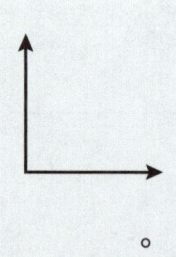

_____ °

6.

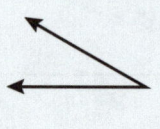

_____ °

Draw angles that have the given measurements.

7. 50°

8. 125°

140

Spectrum Math Grade 4

Name _____

## Lesson 7.16 Finding Missing Angles

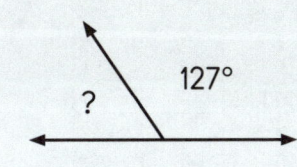

To find the missing angle in a straight angle, subtract the given angle from 180°.

180 − 127 = 53
The missing angle is 53°.

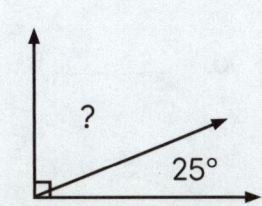

To find the missing angle in a right angle, subtract the given angle from 90°.

90 − 25 = 65
The missing angle is 65°.

**Find the measurement of each missing angle.**

1. 45°   _____°

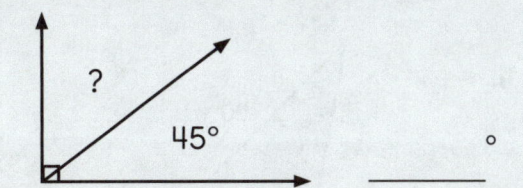

2. 105°   _____°

3. 22°   _____°

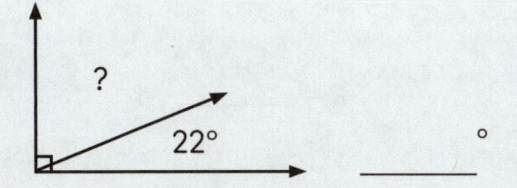

4. 15°   _____°

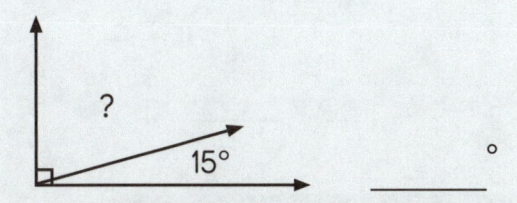

5. 102°   _____°

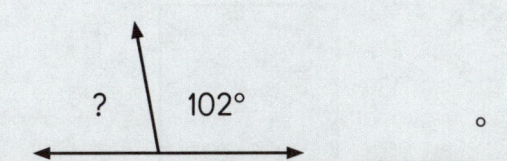

6. 62°   _____°

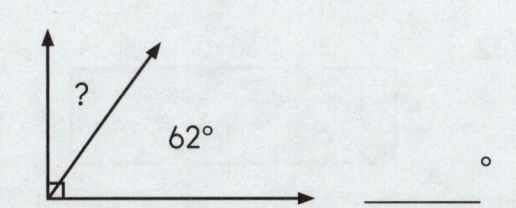

7. 133°   _____°

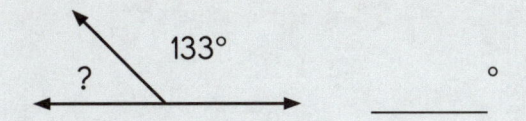

8. 35°   _____°

Spectrum Math Grade 4

141

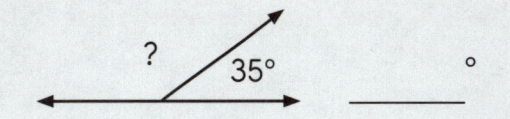

Name _____

## Posttest Chapter 7

**Complete the following conversions.**

1. 4 ft. = _____ in.
2. 5 lb. = _____ oz.
3. 2 T. = _____ lb.

4. 4 qt. = _____ gal.
5. 72 oz. = _____ c.
6. 15 yd. = _____ ft.

7. 5,280 yd. = _____ mi.
8. 7 pt. = _____ c.
9. 80 oz. = _____ lb.

**Find the perimeter of each shape.**

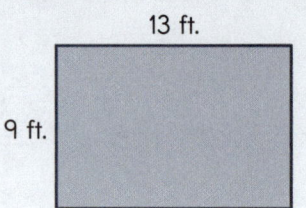

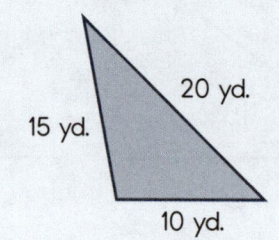

10. 13 ft. / 9 ft.

P = _____ ft.

11. 20 yd., 15 yd., 10 yd.

P = _____ yd.

**Find the area of each shape.**

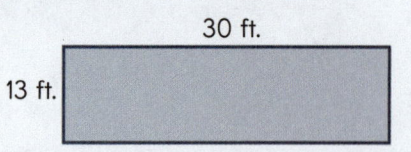

12. 30 ft. / 13 ft.

A = _____ sq. ft.

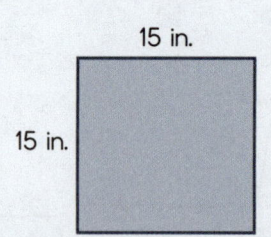

13. 15 in. / 15 in.

A = _____ sq. in.

142

Spectrum Math Grade 4

Name _____

# Posttest Chapter 7

**Solve each problem.**   **Show your work.**

14. Bob ran 75 kilometers this week and 62 kilometers the week before. How many meters did he run over the two weeks?

    Bob ran _____ meters.

15. The local dairy sold 60 pints of milk to one daycare and 40 pints of milk to another daycare. How many cups of milk did the dairy sell to both daycares altogether?

    The dairy sold _____ cups of milk in all.

16. At the store, a container of ice cream weighs 32 ounces. How many pounds do 4 containers of ice cream weigh?

    Four containers weigh _____ pounds.

17. A window measures 16 inches wide and 21 inches tall. What is the area of the window?

    The area of the window is _____ square inches.

Spectrum Math Grade 4

Name _____

## Posttest Chapter 7

**Complete the following conversions.**

18. 600 mm = _____ cm

19. 2,500 L = _____ kL

20. 13 L = _____ mL

21. 4 m = _____ cm

22. 37 km = _____ m

23. 15 L = _____ mL

24. 44 g = _____ mg

25. 9 kg = _____ g

26. 95 m = _____ cm

27. 220 cm = _____ mm

**Use the line plot to answer the questions.**

Length of Sticks in Inches

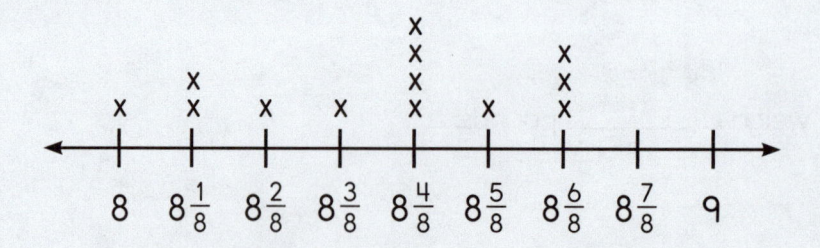

$8 \quad 8\frac{1}{8} \quad 8\frac{2}{8} \quad 8\frac{3}{8} \quad 8\frac{4}{8} \quad 8\frac{5}{8} \quad 8\frac{6}{8} \quad 8\frac{7}{8} \quad 9$

28. How many sticks measure $8\frac{4}{8}$ inches? _____

29. What is the difference between the longest stick measured and the shortest stick measured? _____

Name _____

**Posttest** Chapter 7

Find the measure of each missing angle.

30. 173° ?  _____°

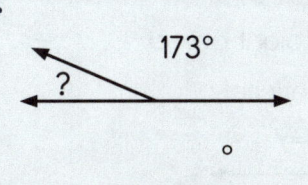

31. ? 42°  _____°

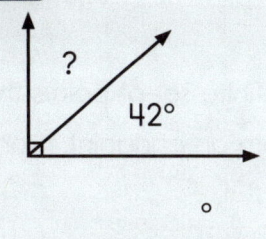

32. 84° ?  _____°

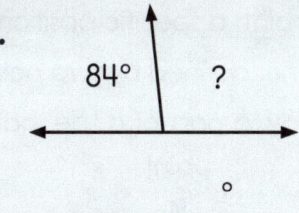

Draw an angle for each given measure.

33. 90°

34. 130°

35. 75°

Measure each angle.

36. _____°

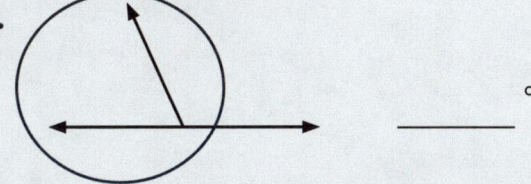

37. _____°

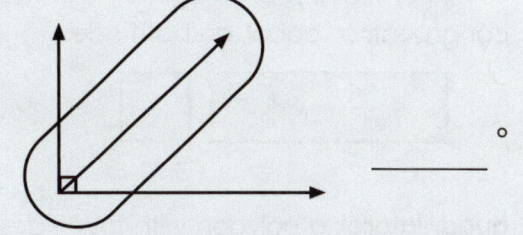

38. _____°

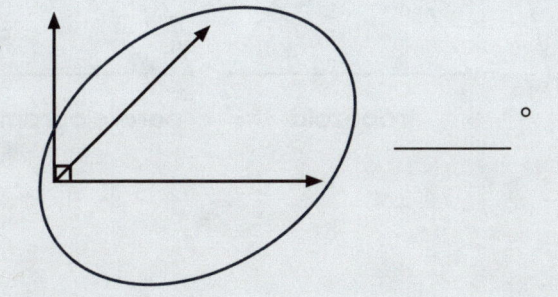

39. _____°

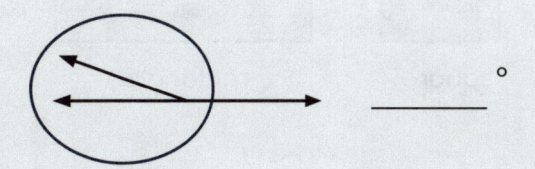

Spectrum Math Grade 4

145

## Chapter 8: Geometry

### Helpful Definitions

**point:** a specific position on a line

**line:** defined by two points, it is an infinite set of points that form a straight object

**ray:** a part of a line that extends from an endpoint in one direction infinitely

point    line    ray

**angle:** the space formed where two rays meet

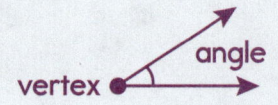

vertex   angle

**vertex:** the point where two rays begin

**parallel lines:** lines that have no points in common and will never intersect

**intersecting lines:** lines that have one point in common

**perpendicular lines:** lines that form right angles where they intersect

parallel lines    intersecting lines    perpendicular lines

**line of symmetry:** an imaginary line that divides a shape or figure into halves that are congruent, or equal, on both sides

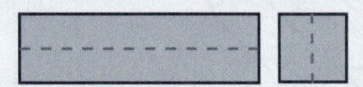

**quadrilateral:** a polygon with four sides:

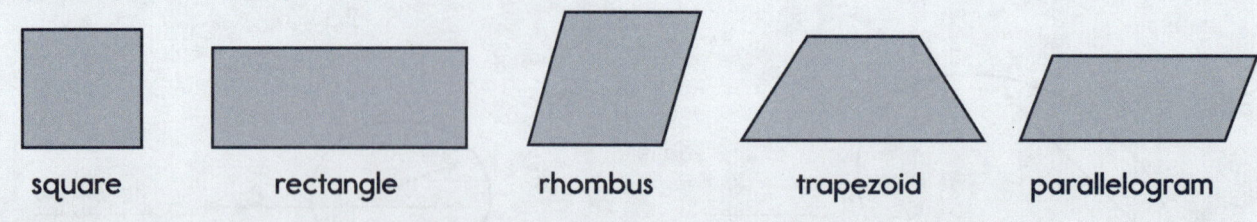

square    rectangle    rhombus    trapezoid    parallelogram

146

Spectrum Math Grade 4

**triangle:** a polygon with three sides

**scalene triangle:** all sides and angles have different measures

**equilateral triangle:** all sides are equal in length; each angle measures 60°

**right triangle:** one angle is 90°

**isosceles triangle:** two congruent sides and two congruent angles

**obtuse triangle:** one angle is more than 90°

## Skills Checklist

☐ Identify and draw points, lines, rays, and angles

☐ Identify and draw parallel, perpendicular, and intersecting lines

☐ Identify and draw lines of symmetry

☐ Identify different types of quadrilaterals and triangles

## Tools and Tips

There is no doubt that shapes and angles are everywhere! From the windows on a home to the roofline of a skyscraper, we can find shapes and angles all around us.

Help your student find shapes and angles. When you see triangles, ask your student to name the type of triangle they see. When you see quadrilaterals (shapes with four sides), ask your student to name the quadrilateral, talk about its angles, or point out the parallel lines on the shape.

Help your student find different types of lines around them. While in the car, point out streets that intersect or run perpendicular to each other. Ask your student to look for examples of parallel lines, such as the lines on a building or sidewalk.

Spectrum Math Grade 4

Name _____

# Pretest Chapter 8

**Name the angles.**

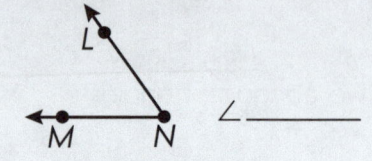

1. ∠ _____

2. 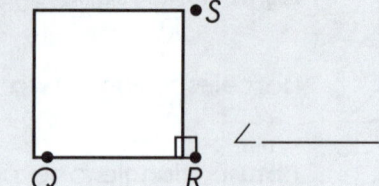 ∠ _____

**Draw each type of line.**

3. parallel

4. perpendicular

5. intersecting

**Draw a line of symmetry for each figure.**

6.

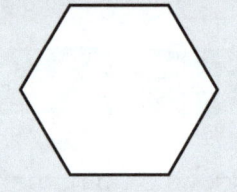

7.

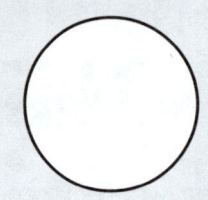

8.

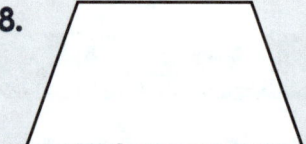

9.

**Identify the quadrilateral.**

10.

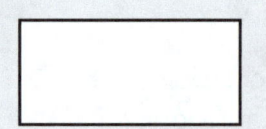

_____

**Identify the triangle.**

11.

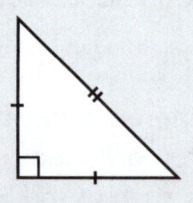

_____

Name _____

# Lesson 8.1 Points, Rays, and Angles

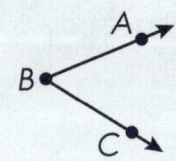

**Angle** *ABC* is made of ray *BA* ($\overrightarrow{BA}$) and ray *BC* ($\overrightarrow{BC}$). The **point** where the two rays begin is called the **vertex**. The vertex (point *B*) is named in the middle of ∠*ABC*.

**Identify the rays and vertex of each angle. Name the angle.**

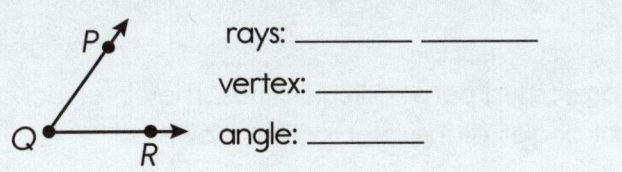

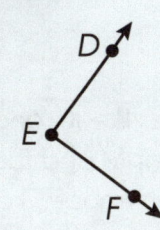

1. rays: _____ _____
   vertex: _____
   angle: _____

2. rays: _____ _____
   vertex: _____
   angle: _____

**Name one angle in each figure shown.**

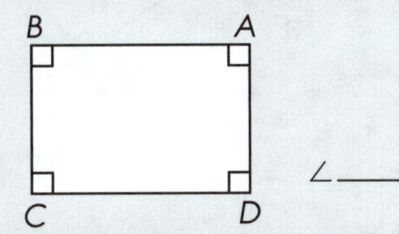

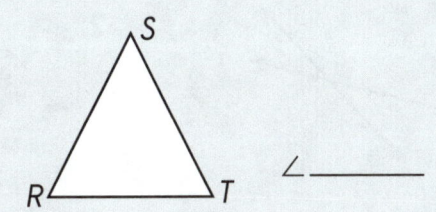

3. ∠ _____

4. ∠ _____

**Draw a figure that contains each angle given.**

5. ∠XYZ

6. ∠UTV

Spectrum Math Grade 4

149

Name _____

# Lesson 8.2 Parallel, Intersecting, and Perpendicular Lines

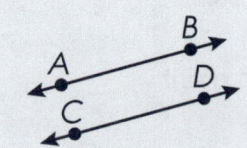

Lines like $\overleftrightarrow{AB}$ and $\overleftrightarrow{CD}$ are called **parallel lines** since they have no points in common. $\overleftrightarrow{AB}$ and $\overleftrightarrow{CD}$ will never intersect.

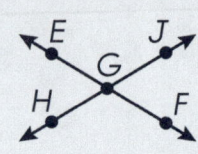

Lines like $\overleftrightarrow{EF}$ and $\overleftrightarrow{HJ}$ are called **intersecting lines**. They have one point in common, point G. $\overleftrightarrow{EF}$ intersects $\overleftrightarrow{HJ}$ at point G.

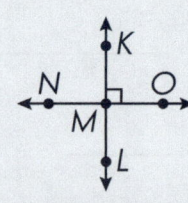

Lines like $\overleftrightarrow{KL}$ and $\overleftrightarrow{NO}$ are called **perpendicular lines**. They intersect at point M and form right angles at the intersection shown by the symbol ⌐ at the angle.

**Identify each pair of lines as *parallel*, *intersecting*, or *perpendicular*.**

1. _____

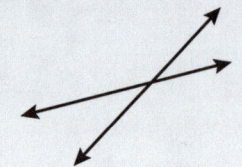

2. _____

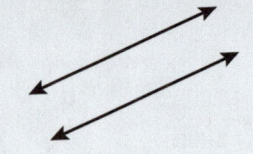

3. _____

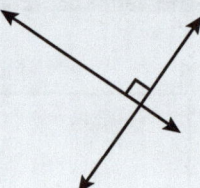

Can you find an example in your home of each type of line? Try it! Draw a picture and write about one example.

_____

_____

_____

_____

Spectrum Math Grade 4

Name _____

# Lesson 8.2 Parallel, Intersecting, and Perpendicular Lines

**Draw an example of each type of lines.**

1. parallel

2. intersecting

3. perpendicular

**List examples of each line type in the figures.**

4. [rectangle ABCD]

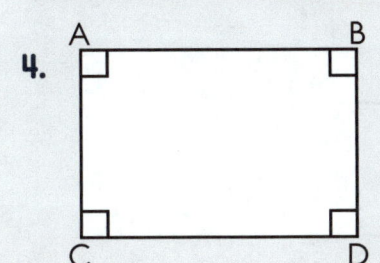

   parallel lines

   _____  _____

   perpendicular lines

   _____  _____

5. [rhombus EFGH]

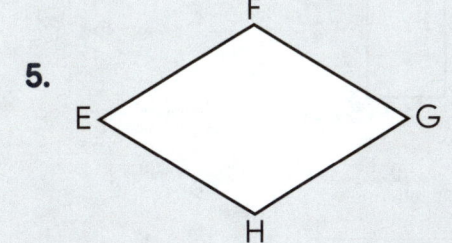

   parallel lines

   _____  _____

6. [right triangle XYZ, right angle at Y]

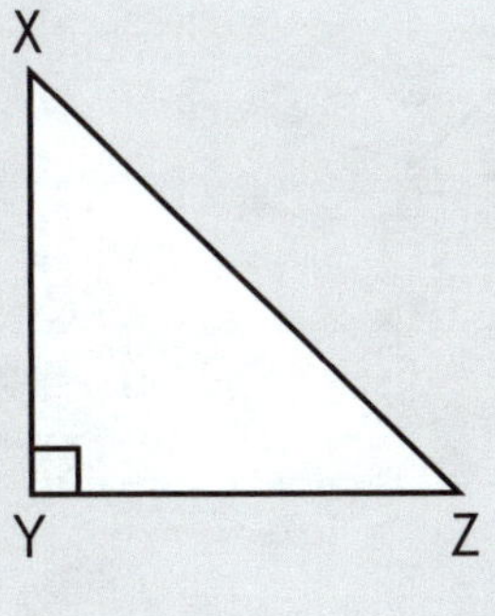

   perpendicular lines

   _____  _____

Spectrum Math Grade 4

151

Name _____

# Lesson 8.3 Symmetrical Shapes

A figure or shape is **symmetrical** when one-half of the figure is the mirror image of the other half.

A **line of symmetry** divides a figure or shape into two halves that are congruent.

A circle is symmetrical.    The letter R is not symmetrical.

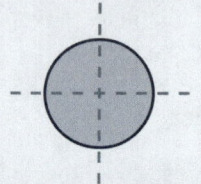

**State whether the line drawn on each figure is a line of symmetry. Write *yes* or *no*.**

1.    _____

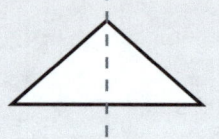

2.    _____

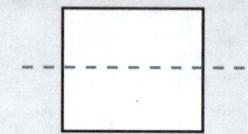

3.    _____

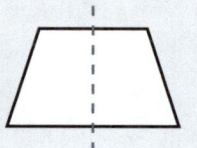

4.    _____

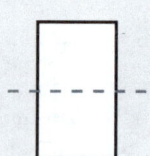

5.    _____

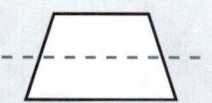

6.    _____

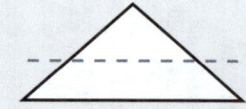

152

Spectrum Math Grade 4

Name _____

# Lesson 8.3 Symmetrical Shapes

**Label each figure as *not symmetrical* or *symmetrical*. If the figure is symmetrical, draw a line of symmetry.**

1. 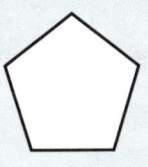 (pentagon)

   _____

2.  (star)

   _____

3. 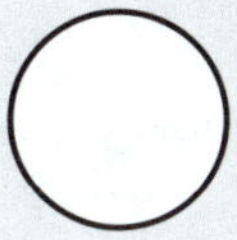 (circle)

   _____

4. 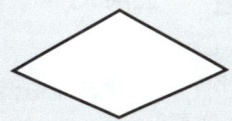 (rhombus)

   _____

5. 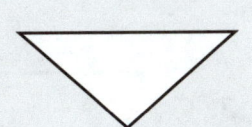 (triangle)

   _____

6.  (square)

   _____

Explain how the lines of symmetry are different for a square than a circle.

_____
_____

Spectrum Math Grade 4

153

Name _____

# Lesson 8.4 Quadrilaterals

A **quadrilateral** is a polygon with four sides. Some examples are square, rectangle, parallelogram, rhombus, kite, and trapezoid.

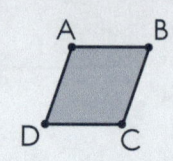

A **parallelogram** has opposite sides that are parallel.
∠DAB = ∠BCD and ∠ADC = ∠CBA     $\overline{AB} = \overline{DC}, \overline{AD} = \overline{BC}$

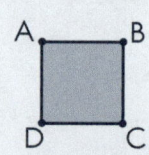

A **square** is a rectangle with four equal-length sides and four right angles.
∠ADC = ∠DCB = ∠CBA = ∠BAD     $\overline{AB} = \overline{BC} = \overline{CD} = \overline{DA}$

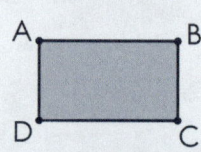

A **rectangle** is a parallelogram with four right angles.
∠ADC = ∠DCB = ∠CBA = ∠BAD     $\overline{AB} = \overline{DC}$ and $\overline{AD} = \overline{BC}$

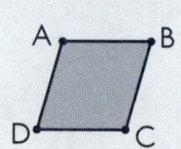

A **rhombus** is a parallelogram that has four equal-length sides. Opposite angles are the same measure.
∠DAB = ∠BCD and ∠ADC = ∠CBA     $\overline{AB} = \overline{DC}, \overline{AD} = \overline{BC}$

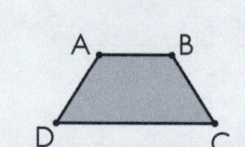

A **trapezoid** has just 2 sides that are parallel: $\overline{AB}$ and $\overline{DC}$.

Identify each quadrilateral with one name from above.

1. _____

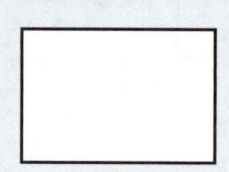

2. _____

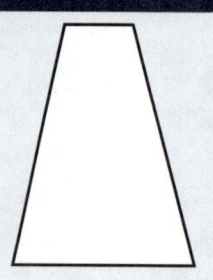

3. _____

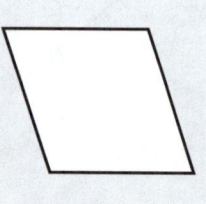

4. _____

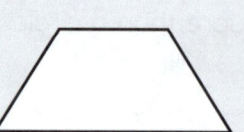

5. _____

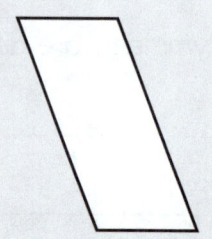

6. _____

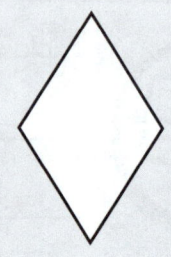

154

Spectrum Math Grade 4

Name _____

# Lesson 8.5 Triangles

A **triangle** is a polygon with 3 sides. Some examples are equilateral, scalene, isosceles, right, obtuse, and acute.

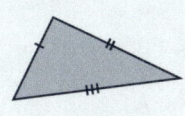

In a **scalene triangle**, all 3 sides have different lengths. Its angles are also all different.

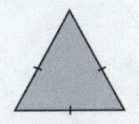

In an **equilateral triangle**, all 3 sides are the same length. All three angles equal 60°.

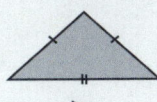

In an **isosceles triangle**, 2 sides have equal lengths. Two of its angles are also equal.

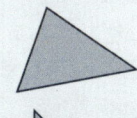

In an **acute triangle**, all angles are less than 90°.

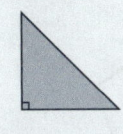

In a **right triangle**, one angle is 90°.

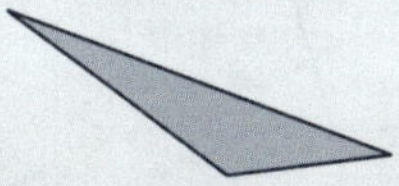

In an **obtuse triangle**, one angle is greater than 90°.

**Identify each triangle with one name from above.**

1. _____

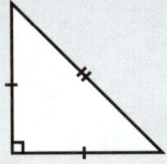

2. _____

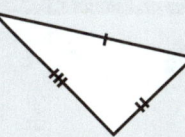

3. _____

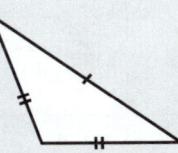

4. _____

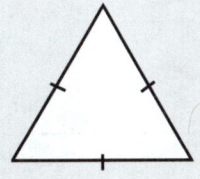

Explain why composing one large triangle from two smaller congruent triangles changes the type of triangle. Give an example.

_____

_____

Spectrum Math Grade 4

155

Name _____

## Posttest Chapter 8

**Draw the line (or lines) of symmetry if the shape is symmetrical.**

1.

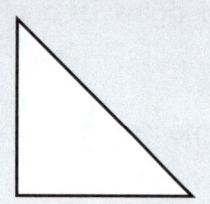

2.

3.

4.

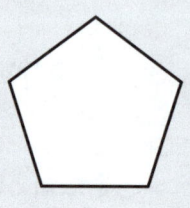

**Identify the lines as parallel, intersecting, or perpendicular.**

5.

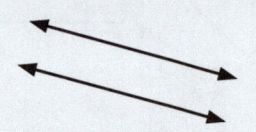

6.

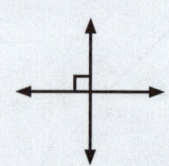

_____

_____

7.

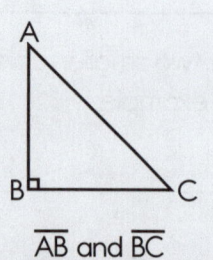

$\overline{AB}$ and $\overline{BC}$

8.

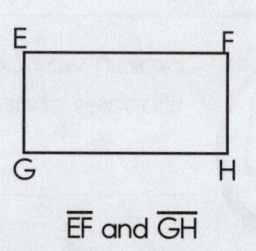

$\overline{EF}$ and $\overline{GH}$

_____

_____

156

Spectrum Math Grade 4

Name _____

# Posttest Chapter 8

**Draw each angle.**

**9.** ∠QRS, right

**10.** ∠DEF, obtuse

**11.** ∠XYZ, acute

**Identify the quadrilateral.**

**12.**

_____

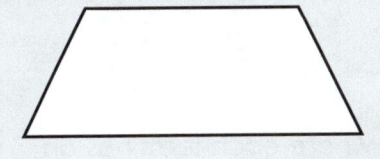

**Identify the triangle.**

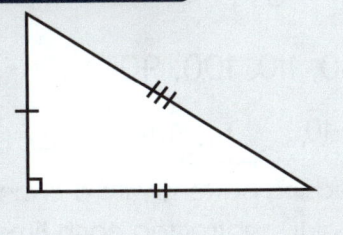

**13.**

_____

Spectrum Math Grade 4

157

# Chapter 9: Preparing for Algebra

## Helpful Definitions

**growing number pattern:** a sequence of numbers that follow a repeating rule or a changing rule; for example, an increasing pattern with repeating rule of +3 looks like this:

3, 6, 9, 12, 15, . . .
+3 +3 +3 +3

An increasing pattern with a changing rule looks like this where each term had one more added to it as the pattern increases:

3, 6, 10, 15, 21, . . .
+3 +4 +5 +6

A decreasing pattern with a repeating rule of −10 looks like this:

120, 110, 100, 90, . . .
−10 −10 −10

A decreasing pattern with a changing rule looks like this where each term has an additional 10 subtracted each time as the pattern decreases:

120, 110, 90, 60, 20, . . .
−10 −20 −30 −40

## Skills Checklist

☐ Complete increasing and decreasing patterns

☐ Analyze the rule of a number pattern

☐ Use a repeating rule to extend a pattern

☐ Use a changing rule to extend a pattern

☐ Solve problems using patterns

## Tools and Tips

Mathematics is filled with patterns. Whether your student is multiplying, adding, subtracting, or counting, there are consistent patterns in the numbers they encounter.

Some number patterns increase or decrease by a given number. For example, in the pattern 5, 8, 11, 14, the numbers increase by 3. Other patterns increase or decrease in a more complicated way. For example, in the pattern 158, 156, 152, 146, the numbers decrease in increments of 2: −2, −4, −6, and so on.

Help your student understand number and shape patterns by giving them a series of numbers or shapes. For example, draw shapes or use shape blocks from home. Have your student complete the pattern that you start.

Name _____

**Pretest** Chapter 9

Write the rule for each pattern.

1. 5, 10, 15, 20, 25, . . . _____

2. 800, 700, 600, 500, . . . _____

3. 1, 2, 4, 8, 16, . . . _____

4. 10,000, 1,000, 100, 10, . . . _____

5. 3, 5, 8, 12, 17, . . . _____

6. 6, 12, 18, 24, . . . _____

Complete the number patterns.

7. 2, 4, 6, 8, _____, _____, _____

8. 80, 70, 60, 50, _____, _____, _____

9. 5, 10, 20, 40, _____, _____, _____

10. 11, 22, 33, 44, _____, _____, _____

# Pretest Chapter 9

**Solve each problem.**   **Show your work.**

**11.** A teacher is handing out pencils to his students. He gave 3 pencils to the first student, 9 pencils to the second student, and 27 pencils to the third student. If this pattern continues, how many pencils will the teacher give the fourth student?

The teacher will give the fourth student _____ pencils.

**12.** A gift shop displays a different number of items in their front window each month. It displayed 13 items in January, 19 items in February, and 25 items in March. If this pattern continues, how many items will the shop display in June?

The gift shop will display _____ items in June.

**13.** Wren is stacking cups in pyramids. Each pyramid has 1 cup at the top. She puts 1 cup in the first pyramid, 3 cups in the second pyramid, and 6 cups in the third pyramid. If the pattern continues, how many cups will be in her sixth stack?

There will be _____ cups in her sixth stack.

Name _____

## Lesson 9.1 Extending Patterns with Addition

To extend a pattern, figure out which operation is used and what number is involved.

We can figure out that each term in the pattern is 2 more than the previous term. The rule is *add 2*, or *+2*. Use the rule to determine the next two terms in the pattern.

1, 3, 5, 7, 9, 11, 13
 +2 +2 +2 +2 +2 +2

**Write the rule for each pattern. Extend the pattern.**

1. 11, 17, 23, _____, _____       Rule: _____

2. 12, 21, 30, _____, _____       Rule: _____

3. 82, 84, 86, _____, _____       Rule: _____

4. 573, 578, 582, _____, _____    Rule: _____

5. 129, 134, 139, _____, _____    Rule: _____

6. 91, 94, 97, _____, _____       Rule: _____

**Draw the next sequence in the pattern.**

7.

162                                                              Spectrum Math Grade 4

Name _____

# Lesson 9.2 Extending Patterns with Subtraction

To extend a pattern, figure out which operation is used and what number is involved.

We can figure out that each term in the pattern is 3 less than the previous term. The rule is *subtract 3*, or –3. Use the rule to determine the next two terms in the pattern.

24, 21, 18, 15, 12, __9__, __6__
 –3 –3 –3 –3 –3 –3

**Write the rule for each pattern. Extend the pattern.**

1. 81, 71, 61, _____, _____    Rule: _____

2. 27, 22, 17, _____, _____    Rule: _____

3. 42, 36, 30, _____, _____    Rule: _____

4. 415, 410, 405, _____, _____    Rule: _____

5. 179, 171, 163, _____, _____    Rule: _____

6. 675, 650, 625, _____, _____    Rule: _____

**Draw the next sequence in the pattern.**

7.

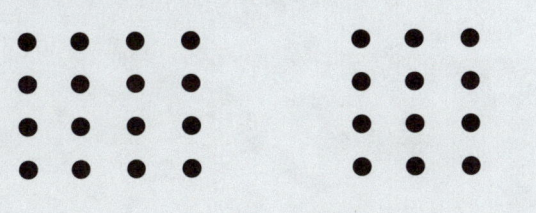

Spectrum Math Grade 4

Name _____

# Lesson 9.3 Extending Patterns with Multiplication

To extend a pattern, figure out which operation is used and what number is involved.

We can figure out that each term in the pattern is 4 times the previous term. The rule is *multiply by 4*, or ×4. Use the rule to determine the next two terms in the pattern.

1, 4, 16, 54, __216__, __864__
×4  ×4  ×4  ×4  ×4

**Write the rule for each pattern. Extend the pattern.**

1. 2, 4, 8, _____, _____     Rule: _____

2. 3, 9, 27, _____, _____     Rule: _____

3. 5, 25, 125, _____, _____     Rule: _____

4. 10, 100, 1,000, _____, _____     Rule: _____

5. 6, 36, 216, _____, _____     Rule: _____

Can you write a pattern whose rule is ×2? Try it! Write at least three terms in the pattern.

164

Spectrum Math Grade 4

Name _____

# Lesson 9.4 Extending Patterns with Division

To extend a pattern, figure out which operation is used and what number is involved.

We can figure out that each term in the pattern is half of the previous term. The rule is *divide by 2*, or ÷2. Use the rule to determine the next two terms in the pattern.

160, 80, 40, 20, __10__, __5__
  ÷2  ÷2  ÷2  ÷2  ÷2

**Write the rule for each pattern. Extend the pattern.**

1. 250, 50, 10, _____    Rule: _____

2. 1,000, 100, 10, _____    Rule: _____

3. 81, 27, 9, _____    Rule: _____

4. 256, 64, 16, _____    Rule: _____

Explain how learning number patterns can help in other areas of math. Give an example.

_____
_____
_____

Spectrum Math Grade 4

165

# Lesson 9.5 Growing Number Patterns with Changing Rules

To find a missing number in a growing pattern with a changing rule:

**Step 1:** Find the difference between the numbers that are next to each other.
**Step 2:** The differences in the number series will show the pattern.
**Step 3:** Add or subtract to find the missing numbers.

**Increasing Pattern**
2, 4, 8, 16, __32__
+2 +4 +8

The differences are 4 − 2 = 2, 8 − 4 = 4, 16 − 8 = 8, etc.
Think: Each number is added to itself to create the increasing pattern.
2 + 2 = 4, 4 + 4 = 8, 8 + 8 = 16, 16 + 16 = ?
The next number in the pattern is 32.

**Decreasing Pattern**
108, 106, 102, 96, 88, __78__
−2 −4 −6 −8

The differences are 108 − 106 = 2, 106 − 102 = 4,
102 − 96 = 6, 96 − 88 = 8, etc.
Think: Count by 2s to get the number for the decreasing pattern.
88 − 10 = 78

**Start with the given number. Extend the pattern according to the rule. The first one has been done for you.**

1. Rule: each term increases by 2 more each time     12, __14__, __18__, __24__, __32__

2. Rule: each term decreases by 1 more each time     85, _____, _____, _____, _____

3. Rule: each term increases by 1 more each time     5, _____, _____, _____, _____

4. Rule: each term decreases by 3 more each time     72, _____, _____, _____, _____

**Circle the term in each pattern that is incorrect. Write the rule.**

5. 6, 11, 17, 23, 32, 41     Rule: _____

6. 95, 85, 76, 68, 60, 55     Rule: _____

166

Spectrum Math Grade 4

Name _____

# Lesson 9.6 Problem Solving

**Solve each problem.**  **Show your work.**

1. Aunt Millie is baking cookies for a bake sale. On Monday she baked 12 cookies. On Tuesday she baked 24 cookies. On Wednesday she baked 36 cookies. If this pattern continues, how many cookies will she bake on Friday?

   Aunt Millie will bake _____ cookies on Friday.

2. Akihiro tries to make a pattern that has the rule *multiply by 4*. He starts with 5 and writes six more terms in the pattern. What would his pattern look like?

   Akihiro's pattern looks like this:

   __5__, _____, _____, _____, _____, _____, _____

3. Tasha sent her friend 3 texts on Monday, 12 texts on Tuesday, and 48 texts on Wednesday. If this pattern continues, how many texts will Tasha send on Thursday?

   Tasha will send _____ texts on Thursday.

4. A tiler is placing tiles in square patterns from one corner of a room. In the first hour, he places 4 tiles. In the second hour he places 9 tiles. In the third hour, he places 16 tiles. If this pattern continues, how many tiles will he place in the fourth hour?

   The tiler will place _____ tiles in the fourth hour.

Spectrum Math Grade 4
167

Name _____

**Posttest** Chapter 9

Write the rule for each pattern.

1. 1, 3, 6, 10, 15, . . .    Rule: _____

2. 1, 2, 4, 7, 11, 16, . . .    Rule: _____

3. 400, 200, 100, 50, . . .    Rule: _____

4. 430, 421, 412, 403, . . .    Rule: _____

Extend each pattern.

5. 7, 9, 11, _____, _____

6. 10, 8, 6, _____, _____

7. 2,304, 576, 144, _____, _____

8. 690, 580, 470, _____, _____

Circle the pattern that matches each rule.

9. Rule: +4     1, 4, 16, 64     203, 207, 211, 215     380, 376, 372, 368

10. Rule: ×2     1, 6, 36, 216     567, 547, 527, 507     11, 22, 44, 88

168

Spectrum Math Grade 4

Name _____

**Posttest** Chapter 9

Solve each problem.    Show your work.

11. A mail carrier is delivering letters to the homes on her route. She puts 4 letters in the first mailbox. She puts 9 letters in the second mailbox. She puts 14 letters in the third mailbox. If this pattern continues, how many letters will she put in the fifth mailbox?

    The mail carrier will put _____ letters in the fifth mailbox.

12. Amad collects rare graphic novels. He visits one bookstore and buys 3 books. He visits a second store and buys 9 books. He visits a third store and buys 16 books. If this pattern continues, how many books will Amad buy at the fourth store?

    Amad will buy _____ books at the fourth store.

13. A mason is building a brick wall. He lays 50 bricks in the first row. If he lays 1 less brick in each row, how many bricks will he lay in the 20th row?

    The mason will lay _____ bricks in the 20th row.

Spectrum Math Grade 4

Name _____

# Learning Checkpoint Chapters 6–9

**To find an equivalent fraction, multiply the fraction by the number in the circle.**

1. $\frac{4}{8}$ = _____ ④

2. $\frac{1}{3}$ = _____ ⑤

**Draw a picture to compare the fractions. Then, write >, <, or =.**

3. $\frac{1}{5}$ ◯ $\frac{2}{10}$

4. $\frac{3}{4}$ ◯ $\frac{5}{8}$

**Add.**

5. $\frac{7}{12} + \frac{3}{12}$ = _____

6. $\frac{4}{8} + \frac{6}{8}$ = _____

**Subtract.**

7. $\frac{3}{5} - \frac{2}{5}$ = _____

8. $\frac{10}{12} - \frac{6}{12}$ = _____

**Decompose the fraction.**

9. $\frac{3}{9}$ = $\frac{\Box}{\Box}$ + $\frac{\Box}{\Box}$ + $\frac{\Box}{\Box}$ or _____ × $\frac{\Box}{\Box}$

**Write the decimal and fraction for each model.**

10.  _____ or _____

11.  _____ or _____

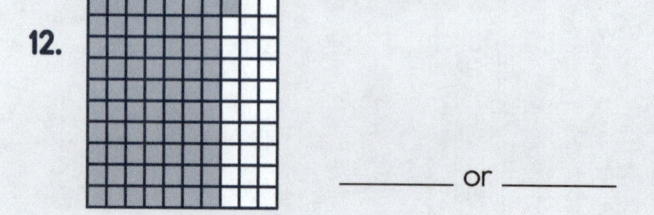

12. _____ or _____

170

Spectrum Math Grade 4

Name _____

# Learning Checkpoint Chapters 6–9

**Add or subtract.**

13. $8\frac{3}{5} + 8\frac{1}{5}$

14. $7\frac{1}{6} + 3\frac{1}{6}$

15. $4\frac{5}{7} - 1\frac{2}{7}$

16. $\frac{4}{10} + \frac{8}{100}$

17. $7\frac{7}{9} - 4\frac{4}{9}$

18. $\frac{2}{10} + \frac{2}{100}$

19. $9\frac{3}{10} + 2\frac{9}{10}$

20. $5\frac{3}{8} + 8\frac{3}{8}$

**Multiply.**

21. $\frac{7}{9} \times 3$

22. $2 \times \frac{1}{10}$

23. $\frac{3}{7} \times 4$

24. $\frac{1}{7} \times 6$

**Complete the following conversions.**

25. 36 inches = _____ yard

26. 8 quarts = _____ gallons

27. 1 cup = _____ ounces

28. 1 mile = _____ yards

29. 2 feet = _____ inches

30. 10 cups = _____ pints

**Find the perimeter and area of each shape.**

31. 30 yd. × 10 yd.

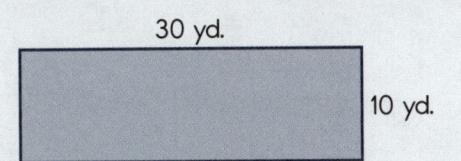

P = _____ yards

A = _____ square yards

32. 12 in. × 6 in.

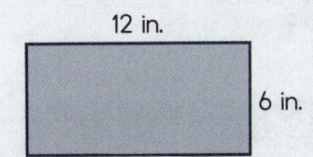

P = _____ inches

A = _____ square inches

Spectrum Math Grade 4

171

Name _____

# Learning Checkpoint Chapters 6–9

**Measure each angle.**

**33.**

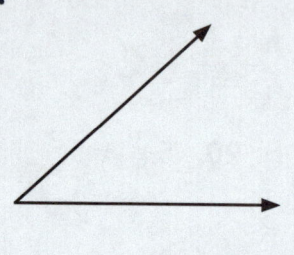

_____ °

**34.**

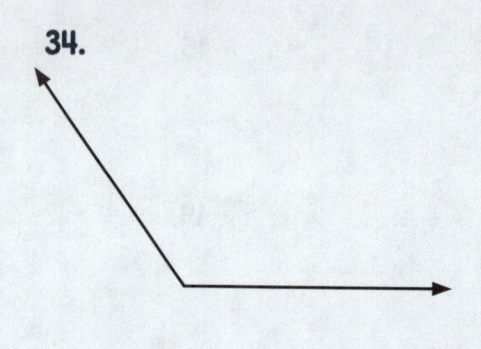

_____ °

**35.**

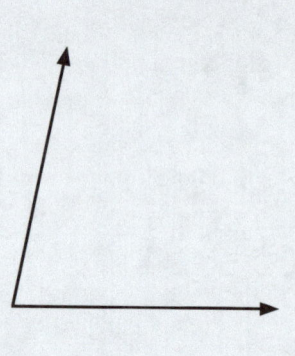

_____ °

**Solve each problem.**

**Show your work.**

**36.** Diego is using a 2-quart container to fill a bucket. If he needs 8 gallons of water to fill the bucket, how many times does he need to fill the 2-quart container?

He needs to fill the container _____ times.

**37.** The clerk measured the length of a piece fabric. The fabric measured 2 yards long. How many feet long is the fabric?

The fabric measured _____ feet long.

**Complete the following conversions.**

**38.** 1 g = _____ mg

**39.** 100 cm = _____ m

**40.** 17 L = _____ mL

172

Spectrum Math Grade 4

Name _____

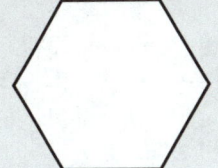

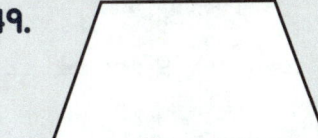

## Learning Checkpoint Chapters 6–9

**Find each missing angle.**

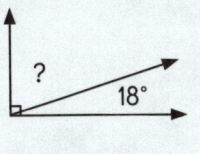

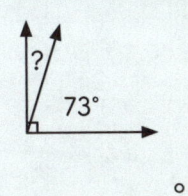

41. ? 18°

_____°

42. ? 73°

_____°

43. ? 81°

_____°

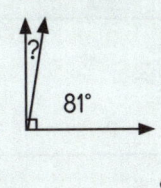

**Name the angles.**

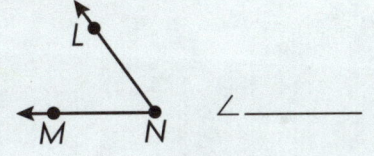

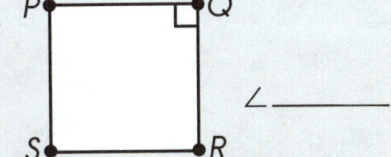

44. L, M, N

∠ _____

45. P, Q, S, R

∠ _____

**Draw each set of lines.**

46. parallel

47. perpendicular

**Draw the line (or lines) of symmetry for each figure.**

48.

49.

Spectrum Math Grade 4

173

Name _____

# Learning Checkpoint Chapters 6–9

**Identify the quadrilateral. Draw a different type of quadrilateral.**

50. [rectangle]

   _____

**Identify the triangle. Draw a different type of triangle.**

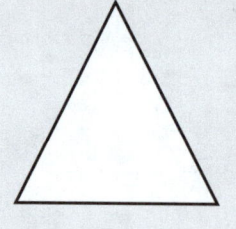

51. [triangle]

   _____

**Write the rule for each pattern. Then, extend the pattern.**

52. 175, 150, 125, 100, 75, _____, _____     Rule: _____

53. 1, 3, 5, 7, 9, _____, _____, _____     Rule: _____

54. 510, 506, 502, _____, _____, _____     Rule: _____

55. 243, 81, 27, _____, _____     Rule: _____

174

Spectrum Math Grade 4

Name _____

# Final Test Chapters 1–9

**Add.**

1.
```
   21
+ 15
```

2.
```
  1,932
+    32
```

3.
```
  718
+  72
```

4.
```
  247
+  38
```

5.
```
   787
+ 193
```

6.
```
  1,005
+    49
```

7.
```
  2,498
+ 1,832
```

8.
```
  6,918
+ 5,832
```

9.
```
   957
+   98
```

10.
```
  2,950
+   709
```

11.
```
  25,765
+  5,403
```

12.
```
  7,864
+ 3,258
```

13.
```
  20,048
   7,212
+    500
```

14.
```
  18,970
+  2,718
```

15.
```
  50,908
   7,312
+  8,903
```

16.
```
  368,174
+   8,310
```

Spectrum Math Grade 4

175

Name _____

# Final Test Chapters 1–9

**Subtract.**

17.  98
    − 7

18.  87
    − 8

19.  54
    − 6

20.  48
    − 9

21.  60
    − 7

22.  705
    −178

23.  6,005
    − 736

24.  7,132
    −5,600

25.  9,568
    −7,432

26.  900
    −445

27.  461
    − 32

28.  1,353
    − 72

Spectrum Math Grade 4

# Final Test Chapters 1–9

**Multiply.**

29.  78 × 9

30.  97 × 9

31.  56 × 8

32.  48 × 8

33.  98 × 98

34.  78 × 15

35.  48 × 36

36.  77 × 54

37.  702 × 6

38.  389 × 8

39.  215 × 8

40.  247 × 2

41.  7,035 × 2

42.  2,003 × 2

43.  3,972 × 8

44.  5,931 × 4

Spectrum Math Grade 4

Name _____

**Final Test** Chapters 1–9

**Multiply.**

45. 3)45    46. 9)72    47. 4)40    48. 5)94

49. 6)493    50. 3)873    51. 7)875    52. 5)987

53. 7)2,598    54. 2)5,282    55. 6)5,631    56. 4)9,637

57. 6)9,832    58. 8)5,000    59. 5)7,004    60. 7)5,111

Name _____

# Final Test Chapters 1–9

**Write each number in expanded form.**

**61.** 2,237 _____

**62.** 397 _____

**63.** 55,608 _____

**64.** 69,735 _____

**Round each number to the place of the underlined number.**

**65.** 103,4̲67 _____  **66.** 1,7̲85,302 _____

**67.** 23̲,451 _____  **68.** 57̲5 _____

**Write >, <, or = to compare each pair of numbers.**

**69.** 325 ◯ 225  **70.** 12,700 ◯ 12,703  **71.** 164,000 ◯ 146,000

**Add or subtract.**

**72.** $\frac{5}{6} + \frac{1}{6} =$ _____  **73.** $\frac{7}{12} - \frac{3}{12} =$ _____  **74.** $\frac{6}{8} + \frac{4}{8} =$ _____

**Complete each equivalent fraction.**

**75.** $\frac{8}{32} = \frac{}{4}$  **76.** $\frac{1}{10} = \frac{}{40}$  **77.** $\frac{5}{100} = \frac{1}{}$

Spectrum Math Grade 4

179

Name _____

# Final Test Chapters 1–9

**Write >, <, or = to compare each pair of fractions.**

78. $\frac{3}{8}$ ◯ $\frac{10}{12}$

79. $\frac{3}{12}$ ◯ $\frac{1}{3}$

80. $\frac{3}{6}$ ◯ $\frac{1}{8}$

**Write the decimal equivalent to the given fraction.**

81. $\frac{8}{10}$ = _____

82. $\frac{7}{100}$ = _____

83. $\frac{3}{10}$ = _____

84. $\frac{65}{100}$ = _____

**Complete the following.**

85. 36 in. = _____ yd.

86. 7 cm = _____ mm

87. 5 T. = _____ lb.

88. 14 km = _____ m

89. 72 kg = _____ g

90. 132 ft. = _____ yd.

**Find the perimeter of each shape.**

91. (triangle with sides 5 ft., 3 ft., 3 ft.)

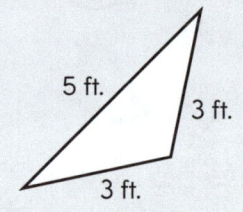

_____ ft.

92. (square with sides 10 in.)

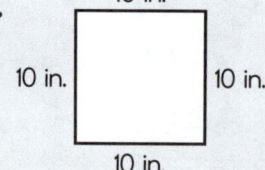

_____ in.

93. (rectangle 15 mm by 7 mm)

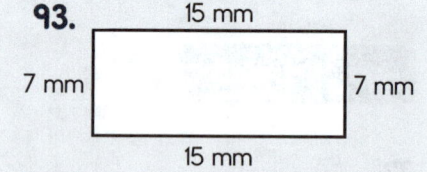

_____ mm

**Find the area of each shape.**

94. (rectangle 30 ft. by 5 ft.)

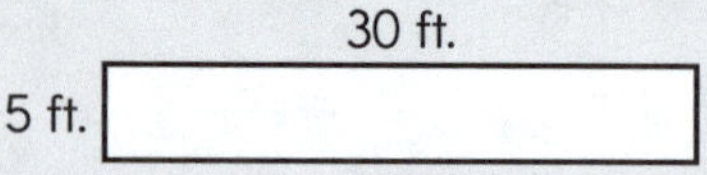

_____ sq. ft.

95. (rectangle 22 cm by 8 cm)

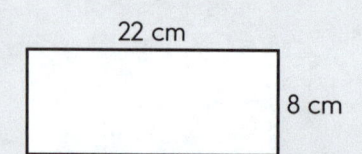

_____ sq. cm

96. (rectangle 10 in. by 30 in.)

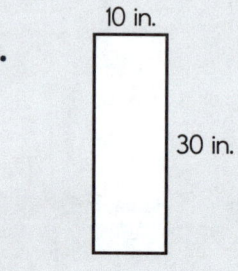

_____ sq. in.

180

Spectrum Math Grade 4

Name _____

# Final Test Chapters 1–9

**Measure each angle.**

97. [angle TUV]  _____°

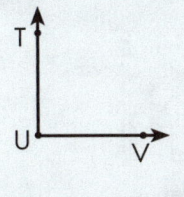

98. [angle HIJ]  _____°

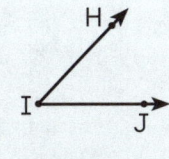

99. [angle LMN]  _____°

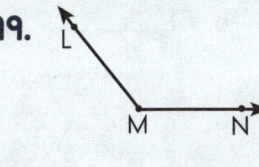

**Draw and label a shape with each given angle.**

100. ∠KLM

101. ∠PQR

102. ∠TUV

**Identify each pair of lines as *parallel*, *intersecting*, or *perpendicular*.**

103. _____

104. _____

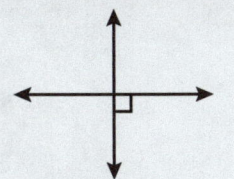

105. _____

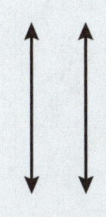

Spectrum Math Grade 4

181

Name _____

# Final Test Chapters 1–9

**Extend each pattern.**

**106.** 45, 48, 51, _____, _____

**107.** 99, 88, 77, 66, _____, _____

**108.** 1,040, 1,030, 1,020, _____, _____

**109.** 25, 75, 125, 175, _____, _____

**Draw a line of symmetry on each symmetrical figure.**

**110.** 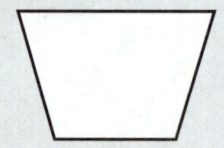   **111.**    **112.** 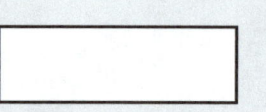    **113.**

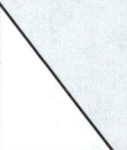

**Add or subtract. Write answers in simplest form.**

**114.** $3\frac{1}{10}$
$+ 4\frac{9}{10}$

**115.** $6\frac{3}{5}$
$- 4\frac{2}{5}$

**116.** $3\frac{3}{4}$
$- 1\frac{1}{4}$

**117.** $1\frac{5}{7}$
$+ 6\frac{4}{7}$

**Multiply.**

**118.** $\frac{8}{9} \times 8$

**119.** $2 \times \frac{7}{12}$

**120.** $7 \times \frac{3}{4}$

**121.** $\frac{4}{7} \times 2$

Name _____

## Scoring Record for Posttests, Learning Checkpoints, and Final Test

Record your test score in the Your Score column. See where your score falls in the Performance columns. Your score is based on the total number of required responses. If your score is fair or needs improvement, review the chapter material.

| Chapter Posttest | Your Score | Performance |  |  |  |
|---|---|---|---|---|---|
|  |  | Excellent | Very Good | Fair | Needs Improvement |
| 1 | ___ of 24 | 22–24 | 19–21 | 17–18 | 16 or fewer |
| 2 | ___ of 30 | 27–30 | 24–26 | 21–23 | 20 or fewer |
| 3 | ___ of 20 | 18–20 | 16–17 | 14–15 | 13 or fewer |
| 4 | ___ of 22 | 20–22 | 18–19 | 16–17 | 15 or fewer |
| 5 | ___ of 24 | 22–24 | 19–21 | 17–18 | 16 or fewer |
| Learning Checkpoint | ___ of 93 | 84–93 | 76–83 | 66–75 | 65 or fewer |
| 6 | ___ of 36 | 33–36 | 29–32 | 26–28 | 25 or fewer |
| 7 | ___ of 39 | 36–39 | 32–35 | 28–31 | 27 or fewer |
| 8 | ___ of 13 | 12–13 | 11 | 10 | 9 or fewer |
| 9 | ___ of 13 | 12–13 | 11 | 10 | 9 or fewer |
| Learning Checkpoint | ___ of 55 | 50–55 | 44–49 | 39–43 | 38 or fewer |
| Final Test | ___ of 121 | 110–121 | 98–109 | 86–97 | 85 or fewer |

Spectrum Math Grade 4

# Answer Key

**AWV:** Answers will vary
**E:** Answer to the enrichment question

## Chapter 1
### Pretest, Pages 8–9
**1.** 19 **2.** 38 **3.** 78 **4.** 49 **5.** 57 **6.** 25 **7.** 69 **8.** 67 **9.** 87 **10.** 77 **11.** 48 **12.** 99 **13.** 13 **14.** 22 **15.** 11 **16.** 52 **17.** 14 **18.** 62 **19.** 41 **20.** 11 **21.** 12 **22.** 52 **23.** 21 **24.** 10 **25.** 24 **26.** 35 **27.** 12 **28.** 9

### Lesson 1.1, Page 10
**1.** 19 **2.** 13 **3.** 29 **4.** 89 **5.** 59 **6.** 97 **7.** 50 **8.** 49 **9.** 61 **10.** 35 **11.** 67 **12.** 68 **13.** 73 **14.** 47 **15.** 99 **E:** You can add the 4 tens and 5 tens to get 9 tens, or 90.

### Lesson 1.2, Page 11
**1.** 21 **2.** 23 **3.** 61 **4.** 65 **5.** 17 **6.** 5 **7.** 11 **8.** 64 **9.** 41 **10.** 81 **11.** 82 **12.** 51 **13.** 22 **14.** 4 **15.** 92 **16.** 50

### Lesson 1.3, Page 12
**1.** 12 **2.** 11 **3.** 15 **4.** 16 **5.** 17 **6.** 19 **7.** 17 **8.** 14 **9.** 18 **10.** 10 **11.** 14 **12.** 19 **13.** 12 **14.** 17 **15.** 18

### Lesson 1.4, Page 13
**1.** 65 **2.** 91 **3.** 74 **4.** 81 **5.** 47 **6.** 34 **7.** 75 **8.** 72 **9.** 63 **10.** 62 **11.** 80 **12.** 92 **13.** 80 **14.** 90 **15.** 93 **16.** 56

### Lesson 1.5, Page 14
**1.** 102 **2.** 163 **3.** 194 **4.** 245 **5.** 167 **6.** 139 **7.** 208 **8.** 170 **9.** 276 **10.** 115 **11.** 260 **12.** 144

### Lesson 1.5, Page 15
**1.** 106 **2.** 115 **3.** 169 **4.** 104 **5.** 139 **6.** 138 **7.** 170 **8.** 105 **9.** 231 **10.** 222 **11.** 123 **12.** 227 **13.** 175 **14.** 166 **15.** 175 **16.** 212 **E:** AWV

### Lesson 1.6, Page 16
**1.** 137 **2.** 115 **3.** 109 **4.** 105 **5.** 118 **6.** 109 **7.** 118 **8.** 105 **9.** 108 **10.** 119 **11.** 112 **12.** 146 **13.** 115 **14.** 143 **15.** 86 **16.** 119

### Lesson 1.6, Page 17
**1.** 178 **2.** 88 **3.** 277 **4.** 69 **5.** 92 **6.** 267 **7.** 87 **8.** 186 **9.** 358 **10.** 86 **11.** 442 **12.** 181 **E:** You must subtract the ones first so that you can regroup from the larger place values.

### Lesson 1.7, Page 18
**1.** 79 **2.** 82 **3.** 62 **4.** 43 **5.** 90 **6.** 55 **7.** 71 **8.** 75 **9.** 213 **10.** 161 **11.** 141 **12.** 166

### Lesson 1.8, Page 19
**1.** 54 **2.** 6 **3.** 19 **4.** 58 **5.** 34 **6.** 11 **7.** 41 **8.** 17 **9.** 79 **10.** 97 **11.** 85 **12.** 127

### Lesson 1.9, Page 20
**1.** 64 **2.** 5 **3.** 12 **4.** 28 **5.** 127 **6.** 57 **7.** 212 **8.** 575 **9.** 335

### Lesson 1.10, Page 21
**1.** 86 **2.** 166 **3.** 137 **4.** 335

### Posttest, Pages 22–23
**1.** 53 **2.** 100 **3.** 67 **4.** 165 **5.** 306 **6.** 204 **7.** 121 **8.** 480 **9.** 104 **10.** 44 **11.** 211 **12.** 192 **13.** 73 **14.** 72 **15.** 18 **16.** 89 **17.** 189 **18.** 144 **19.** 145 **20.** 323 **21.** 100 **22.** 32 **23.** 52 **24.** 200

## Chapter 2
### Pretest, Pages 26–27
**1.** 50 + 1 **2.** 900 + 70 + 3 **3.** 2,000 + 600 + 70 + 5 **4.** 1,000 + 200 + 60 + 5 **5.** 80,000 + 4,000 + 700 + 40 **6.** 700,000 + 90,000 + 30 + 6 **7.** nine hundred forty-five **8.** four thousand three hundred thirty-seven **9.** fifty-two thousand eighty-two **10.** six hundred twenty-eight thousand four hundred **11.** four hundred ninety-six thousand five hundred twenty-nine **12.** three hundred sixty-seven thousand four hundred fourteen **13.** < **14.** > **15.** < **16.** < **17.** > **18.** > **19.** < **20.** > **21.** = **22.** 900 **23.** 8,000 **24.** 1,680 **25.** 80,000 **26.** 732,000

184

Spectrum Math Grade 4

# Answer Key

**27.** 600,000 **28.** 10,000 **29.** 10 **30.** 100,000 **31.** 1 **32.** 100 **33.** 10,000

## Lesson 2.1, Page 28

**1.** 400 + 30 **2.** 500 + 40 + 9 **3.** 700 + 10 + 5 **4.** 600 + 8 **5.** 200 + 1 **6.** 900 + 7 **7.** 500 + 50 + 4 **8.** 300 + 10 + 2 **9.** 132 **10.** 513 **11.** 87 **12.** eight hundred fifty-two **13.** one hundred nineteen **14.** five hundred ninety-five **15.** 70 **16.** 900 **17.** 3 **18.** 90

## Lesson 2.2, Page 29

**1.** 600,000 + 50,000 + 3,000 + 400 + 10 **2.** 70,000 + 6,000 + 900 + 80 + 2 **3.** 100,000 + 3,000 + 200 + 30 + 4 **4.** 100,000 + 90,000 + 9,000 + 400 + 80 + 2 **5.** 30,000 + 2,000 + 400 + 50 + 1 **6.** 8,000 + 400 + 30 **7.** eighty-five thousand thirty-four **8.** eleven thousand nine hundred eighty-seven **9.** one hundred fifty-three thousand seven hundred twenty-one **10.** nine hundred sixty-eight thousand four hundred twenty-five **11.** 5 **12.** 9 **13.** 9 **14.** 4 **15.** 6 **16.** 2 **E:** The expanded form of 2,007 has only two addends whereas 2,397 has four addends.

## Lesson 2.3, Page 30

**1.** 6,420 **2.** 5,880 **3.** 45,290 **4.** 980 **5.** 67,500 **6.** 4,400 **7.** 8,600 **8.** 79,300 **9.** 74,000 **10.** 3,000 **11.** 62,000 **12.** 10,000

## Lesson 2.3, Page 31

**1.** 180,000 **2.** 740,000 **3.** 30,000 **4.** 640,000 **5.** 700,000 **6.** 200,000 **7.** 400,000 **8.** 600,000 **E:** Look at the digit to the right of the place you are rounding too. If it is 4 or less, round down. If it is 5 or more, round up.

## Lesson 2.4, Page 32

**1.** < **2.** > **3.** < **4.** > **5.** < **6.** > **7.** > **8.** < **9.** = **10.** > **11.** < **12.** <

## Lesson 2.4, Page 33

**1–10.** AWV **11.** < **12.** > **13.** > **14.** < **15.** = **16.** < **E:** AWV

## Posttest, Pages 34–35

**1.** 900,000 + 60,000 + 5,000 + 10 + 2 **2.** 600,000 + 90,000 + 3,000 + 100 + 40 + 5 **3.** 100,000 + 3,000 + 400 + 50 + 8 **4.** 20,000 + 3,000 + 900 + 70 + 2 **5.** 400,000 + 70,000 + 1,000 + 400 + 40 **6.** 10,000 + 8,000 + 300 + 20 + 1 **7.** five thousand twelve **8.** one hundred two **9.** one thousand one hundred forty-one **10.** ninety-nine thousand six hundred twelve **11.** eight hundred thirty-four thousand seven hundred sixty-three **12.** twenty-one thousand eight hundred seventeen **13.** 5,000 **14.** 8,000 **15.** 1,000 **16.** 99,000 **17.** 835,000 **18.** 22,000 **19.** 700,00 **20.** 200,000 **21.** 500,000 **22.** 500,000 **23.** 500,000 **24.** 400,000 **25.** < **26.** < **27.** > **28.** < **29.** < **30.** <

# Chapter 3
## Pretest, Pages 38–39

**1.** 779 **2.** 1,971 **3.** 927 **4.** 6,930 **5.** 5,720 **6.** 2,047 **7.** 3,588 **8.** 1,877 **9.** 6,000 **10.** 6,737 **11.** 4,790 **12.** 3,998 **13.** 553 **14.** 542 **15.** 408 **16.** 605 **17.** 2,281 **18.** 1,163 **19.** 5,381 **20.** 8,122 **21.** 3,967 **22.** 1,318 **23.** 5,905 **24.** 2,413 **25.** 5,330 **26.** 406 **27.** 245 **28.** 448

## Lesson 3.1, Page 40

**1.** 909 **2.** 750 **3.** 589 **4.** 259 **5.** 788 **6.** 993 **7.** 561 **8.** 505 **9.** 720 **10.** 983 **11.** 810 **12.** 900 **13.** 584 **14.** 397 **15.** 1,098 **16.** 352

## Lesson 3.2, Page 41

**1.** 625 **2.** 151 **3.** 69 **4.** 412 **5.** 1,311 **6.** 6,300 **7.** 5,032 **8.** 2,108 **9.** 4,327 **10.** 6,364 **11.** 1,957 **12.** 4,064 **13.** 3,446 **14.** 7,606 **15.** 4,382 **16.** 6,372

Spectrum Math Grade 4

# Answer Key

## Lesson 3.3, Page 42
**1.** 2,897 **2.** 4,866 **3.** 7,284 **4.** 3,661 **5.** 5,115 **6.** 3,737 **7.** 5,908 **8.** 7,760 **9.** 10,100 **10.** 7,983 **11.** 4,790 **12.** 3,776 **13.** 7,113 **14.** 9,824 **15.** 3,477 **16.** 5,950

## Lesson 3.4, Page 43
**1.** 5,949 **2.** 7,077 **3.** 920 **4.** 3,158

## Lesson 3.5, Page 44
**1.** 20,115 **2.** 69,600 **3.** 33,998 **4.** 62,422 **5.** 78,064 **6.** 27,680 **7.** 81,999 **8.** 89,341

## Lesson 3.5, Page 45
**1.** 65,111 **2.** 12,999 **3.** 15,142 **4.** 33,650 **5.** 7,025 **6.** 14,009 **7.** 23,605 **8.** 52,108 **9.** 32,899 **10.** 16,998 **11.** 10,890 **12.** 22,749 **13.** 19,115 **14.** 23,998 **15.** 19,070 **16.** 87,732 **E:** Add or subtract 1 from both numbers, then solve.

## Lesson 3.6, Page 46
**1.** 730 **2.** 910 **3.** 1,068 **4.** 807 **5.** 1,272 **6.** 2,275 **7.** 9,974 **8.** 4,594 **9.** 9,204 **10.** 7,199 **11.** 12,820 **12.** 16,661

## Lesson 3.7, Page 47
**1.** 12,598 **2.** 10,909 **3.** 6,624 **4.** 3,860 **5.** 29,850 **6.** 22,871 **7.** 16,516 **8.** 48,390 **9.** 91,001 **10.** 40,305 **11.** 51,510 **12.** 65,237 **13.** 30,583 **14.** 27,509 **15.** 91,216 **16.** 100,124

## Lesson 3.8, Page 48
**1.** 62 **2.** 15,400 **3.** 4,724 **4.** 40,851

## Lesson 3.9, Page 49
**1.** 2,727 **2.** 20,039 **3.** 78,012 **4.** 12,000 **5.** 3,476 **6.** 1,783 **7.** 11,723 **8.** 2,325 **9.** 3,556 **10.** 1,198 **11.** 5,191 **12.** 786 **13.** 49,106 **14.** 73,960 **15.** 23,660 **16.** 9,791 **E:** If the digits in a column add to greater than 9, you will have to regroup.

## Lesson 3.9, Page 50
**1.** 7,263 **2.** 2,470 **3.** 8,675 **4.** 15,865 **5.** 1,009 **6.** 250 **7.** 1,243 **8.** 884 **9.** 73,794 **10.** 20,470 **11.** 133,397 **12.** 121,344 **13.** 3,988 **14.** 2,567 **15.** 2,075 **16.** 18,354 **17.** 42,606 **18.** 7,372 **19.** 6,781 **20.** 42,050

## Lesson 3.10, Page 51
**1.** 111,753 **2.** 14,125 **3.** 4,730 **4.** 2,869

## Posttest, Pages 52–53
**1.** 10,050 **2.** 51,609 **3.** 1,293 **4.** 1,417 **5.** 7,835 **6.** 3,459 **7.** 5,909 **8.** 6,742 **9.** 19,991 **10.** 991 **11.** 4,232 **12.** 5,218 **13.** 42,753 **14.** 22,431 **15.** 24,023 **16.** 28,606 **17.** 1,028 **18.** 1,470 **19.** 11,808 **20.** 3,185

# Chapter 4
## Pretest, Pages 56–57
**1.** 56 **2.** 75 **3.** 1,208 **4.** 85 **5.** 90 **6.** 144 **7.** 14,805 **8.** 261 **9.** 4,732 **10.** 1,056 **11.** 2,821 **12.** 1,544 **13.** 24,200 **14.** 68,859 **15.** 22,880 **16.** 1, 2, 3, 4, 6, 12; composite **17.** 1, 2, 4, 5, 10, 20; composite **18.** 1, 11; prime **19.** 1, 2, 4, 8, 16, 32; composite **20.** 1, 5; prime **21.** 250 **22.** 198 **23.** 2,145 **24.** 50

## Lesson 4.1, Page 58
**1.** 1, 2, 4, 8, 16, 32, 64; composite **2.** 1, 43; prime **3.** 1, 53; prime **4.** 1, 2, 3, 4, 6, 8, 9, 12, 18, 24, 36, 72; composite **5.** 1, 19; prime **6.** 1, 2, 3, 4, 6, 8, 12, 16, 24, 48; composite **7.** 1, 2, 11, 22; composite **8.** 1, 2, 3, 4, 6, 9, 12, 18, 36; composite **9.** 1, 89; prime **10.** 1, 31; prime **11.** 1, 2, 4, 5, 8, 10, 16, 20, 40, 80; composite **12.** 1, 5, 11, 55; composite

# Answer Key

### Lesson 4.1, Page 59

| 1 | 2 | 3 | 4 | 5 | 6 | 7 | 8 | 9 | 10 |
|---|---|---|---|---|---|---|---|---|----|
| 11 | 12 | 13 | 14 | 15 | 16 | 17 | 18 | 19 | 20 |
| 21 | 22 | 23 | 24 | 25 | 26 | 27 | 28 | 29 | 30 |
| 31 | 32 | 33 | 34 | 35 | 36 | 37 | 38 | 39 | 40 |
| 41 | 42 | 43 | 44 | 45 | 46 | 47 | 48 | 49 | 50 |
| 51 | 52 | 53 | 54 | 55 | 56 | 57 | 58 | 59 | 60 |
| 61 | 62 | 63 | 64 | 65 | 66 | 67 | 68 | 69 | 70 |
| 71 | 72 | 73 | 74 | 75 | 76 | 77 | 78 | 79 | 80 |
| 81 | 82 | 83 | 84 | 85 | 86 | 87 | 88 | 89 | 90 |
| 91 | 92 | 93 | 94 | 95 | 96 | 97 | 98 | 99 | 100 |

**E:** False because 7 × 9 = 21 and 9 × 9 = 81.

### Lesson 4.2, Page 60
**1.** 42 **2.** 150 **3.** 165 **4.** 63

### Lesson 4.3, Page 61
**1.** 46 **2.** 71 **3.** 48 **4.** 66 **5.** 70 **6.** 88 **7.** 86 **8.** 90 **9.** 88 **10.** 36 **11.** 48 **12.** 28 **13.** 99 **14.** 90 **15.** 84 **16.** 77

### Lesson 4.4, Page 62
**1.** 292 **2.** 50 **3.** 108 **4.** 260 **5.** 92 **6.** 38 **7.** 52 **8.** 204 **9.** 270 **10.** 376 **11.** 288 **12.** 384 **13.** 156 **14.** 136 **15.** 126 **16.** 165

### Lesson 4.5, Page 63
**1.** 141 **2.** 188 **3.** 115 **4.** 368

### Lesson 4.6, Page 64
**1.** 354 **2.** 1,220 **3.** 1,120 **4.** 456 **5.** 1,400 **6.** 685 **7.** 981 **8.** 316 **9.** 1,410 **10.** 1,278 **11.** 1,740 **12.** 1,161 **13.** 1,675 **14.** 1,330 **15.** 3,368 **16.** 1,809

### Lesson 4.7, Page 65
**1.** 726 **2.** 495 **3.** 800 **4.** 713

### Lesson 4.8, Page 66
**1.** 418 **2.** 2,496 **3.** 700 **4.** 2,310 **5.** 957 **6.** 1,311 **7.** 1,105 **8.** 1,936 **9.** 3,458 **10.** 935 **11.** 1,012 **12.** 1,496 **E:** AWV but should include 54 × 12 = 648. Then, add four zeros to the end of the number to get 6,480,000.

### Lesson 4.9, Page 67
**1.** 9,450 **2.** 22,134 **3.** 6,027 **4.** 6,270 **5.** 13,821 **6.** 4,480 **7.** 4,508 **8.** 61,916 **9.** 26,016 **10.** 24,160 **11.** 47,771 **12.** 37,800 **13.** 14,058 **14.** 29,754 **15.** 59,711 **16.** 30,366

### Lesson 4.10, Page 68
**1.** 30,765 **2.** 35,480 **3.** 6,108 **4.** 26,605 **5.** 18,886 **6.** 31,780 **7.** 22,659 **8.** 43,584 **9.** 11,045 **10.** 48,690 **11.** 12,956 **12.** 26,190

### Lesson 4.11, Page 69
**1.** 96 **2.** 396 **3.** 750 **4.** 240

### Posttest, Pages 70–71
**1.** 288 **2.** 192 **3.** 798 **4.** 726 **5.** 4,501 **6.** 23,919 **7.** 17,886 **8.** 21,400 **9.** 4,800 **10.** 391 **11.** 10,608 **12.** 6,288 **13.** 1, 5, 17, 85; composite **14.** 1, 59; prime **15.** 1, 3, 5, 15; composite **16.** 1, 2, 13, 26; composite **17.** 1, 2, 5, 7, 10, 14, 35, 70; composite **18.** 1, 2, 17, 34; composite **19.** 252 **20.** 14,880 **21.** 805 **22.** 180

### Chapter 5
### Pretest, Pages 74–75
**1.** 5 **2.** 7 **3.** 3 **4.** 9 **5.** 5 **6.** 6 **7.** 6 **8.** 9 **9.** 8 **10.** 10 **11.** 21 **12.** 20 r1 **13.** 300 **14.** 442 r4 **15.** 938 r3 **16.** 2,154 **17.** 4 **18.** 8 **19.** 15 **20.** 47

### Lesson 5.1, Page 76
**1.** 100 **2.** 10 **3.** 10 **4.** 10 **5.** 10 **6.** 100 **7.** 100 **8.** 10 **9.** 60 **10.** 4 **11.** 20 **12.** 9

Spectrum Math **Grade 4**

# Answer Key

## Lesson 5.2, Page 77
1. 7 2. 4 3. 9 4. 6 5. 5 6. 9 7. 5 8. 4 9. 9 10. 9 11. 8
12. 8 13. 5 14. 6 15. 7 E: Multiply the quotient by the divisor. The answer should match the dividend.

## Lesson 5.3, Page 78
1. 7 2. 5 3. 6 4. 8 5. 7 6. 10 7. 6 8. 8 9. 9 10. 8 11. 8
12. 6 13. 2 14. 7 15. 8 E: 7 × 6 = 42 or 6 × 7 = 42

## Lesson 5.4, Page 79
1. 8 2. 5 3. 3 4. 8 5. 4 6. 6 7. 7 8. 7 9. 6 10. 8 11. 5
12. 6 13. 2 14. 4 15. 7

## Lesson 5.5, Page 80
1. 7 2. 4 3. 9 4. 7 5. 6 6. 8 7. 6 8. 9 9. 4 10. 9 11. 6
12. 7 13. 9 14. 8 15. 8 16. 4 17. 3 18. 7 19. 8 20. 4

## Lesson 5.6, Page 81
1. 8 2. 5 3. 9 4. 3

## Lesson 5.7, Page 82
1. 5 r1 2. 8 r1 3. 7 r3 4. 9 5. 5 r5 6. 8 r2 7. 5 r2
8. 6 r1 9. 7 r1 10. 6 r4 11. 3 r3 12. 8 r1 13. 3 r1 14. 9 r1
15. 8 r1 16. 2 r4

## Lesson 5.7, Page 83
1. 18 2. 15 r1 3. 19 r3 4. 24 5. 17 r1 6. 32 7. 12 r3 8. 12
9. 15 r3 10. 11 r1 11. 22 12. 19 r2 13. 11 r5 14. 25 15. 11
16. 13 r2

## Lesson 5.8, Page 84
1. 90 2. 81 r3 3. 41 r3 4. 43 r1 5. 92 6. 46 r1 7. 62
8. 108 r8

## Lesson 5.8, Page 85
1. 128 r5 2. 449 3. 141 r2 4. 130 r1 5. 158 r1 6. 183
7. 109 r8 8. 128 r1 9. 324 10. 197 11. 105 r4 12. 112 r1
13. 261 r1 14. 157 r3 15. 225 r1 16. 174

## Lesson 5.9, Page 86
1. 1,306 2. 1,720 r3 3. 2,065 r3 4. 876 r5 5. 1,036 r3
6. 2,460 r1 7. 1,132 r5 8. 2,121

## Lesson 5.9, Page 87
1. 1,195 r3 2. 301 r3 3. 2,431 4. 4,565 r1 5. 639 r2
6. 3,320 r1 7. 491 r3 8. 2,807 9. 538 10. 1,264
11. 7,293 12. 2,121 r2

## Lesson 5.10, Page 88
1. 8 2. 38 3. 53, 2 4. 730

## Lesson 5.10, Page 89
1. 116, 7 2. 68 3. 17

## Posttest, Pages 90–91
1. 6 2. 3 3. 8 4. 10 5. 8 6. 6 7. 2 8. 3 9. 5 10. 4 r2
11. 6 12. 7 13. 48 14. 29 15. 11 r5 16. 4 r3 17. 183 r2
18. 127 19. 100 20. 2,039 r1 21. 8 22. 3 23. 8 24. 65

## Learning Checkpoint Chapters 1–5, Pages 92–97
1. 19 2. 74 3. 89 4. 59 5. 31 6. 71 7. 10 8. 53 9. 66
10. 84 11. 8 12. 19 13. 69 14. 59 15. 82 16. 99 17. 302
18. 692 19. 209 20. 389 21. 700 + 30 + 2 22. 60,000
+ 4,000 + 100 23. 4,000 + 700 + 90 24. 1,000 + 3
25. 300,000 + 10,000 + 4,000 + 700 + 30 + 2
26. 50,000 + 20 27. 13,600 28. 80,000 29. 933,000
30. > 31. < 32. < 33. = 34. > 35. > 36. 875 37. 783
38. 7,941 39. 3,032 40. 29,014 41. 4,095 42. 16,949
43. 39,087 44. 5,150 45. 10,990 46. 4,970 47. 8,378
48. 91,710 49. 110,811 50. 83,77 51. 79,967 52. 56
53. 36 54. 28 55. 48 56. 84 57. 256 58. 28 59. 88
60. 48 61. 80 62. 336 63. 576 64. 420 65. 175
66. 441 67. 110 68. 242 69. 992 70. 860 71. 500
72. 820 73. 1,875 74. 576 75. 2,997 76. 2,040
77. 18,810 78. 16,000 79. 9,353 80. 13,294 81. 46,124
82. 9 83. 8 84. 8 85. 8 86. 6 87. 100 88. 321 89. 103
90. 36 91. 60 92. 210 93. 18

# Answer Key

## Chapter 6
### Pretest, Pages 100–101
1. $\frac{12}{24}$ 2. $\frac{10}{15}$ 3. $\frac{6}{36}$ 4. $\frac{9}{27}$ 5. Drawings will vary. =
6. Drawings will vary. > 7. $\frac{10}{10}$ or 1 8. $\frac{7}{8}$ 9. $\frac{2}{5}$ 10. $\frac{3}{12}$ or $\frac{1}{4}$ 11. $\frac{1}{4} + \frac{1}{4}$, 2, $\frac{1}{4}$ 12. 0.5 or $\frac{5}{10}$ 13. 0.1 or $\frac{1}{10}$
14. 0.44 or $\frac{44}{100}$ 15. $\frac{48}{100}$ 16. $10\frac{2}{6}$ or $10\frac{1}{3}$ 17. $13\frac{6}{8}$
18. $16\frac{4}{5}$ 19. $3\frac{3}{9}$ 20. $\frac{22}{100}$ 21. $12\frac{2}{10}$ 22. $3\frac{19}{56}$ 23. $1\frac{6}{10}$
24. $\frac{32}{9}$ 25. $\frac{3}{8}$ 26. $\frac{8}{7}$ 27. $\frac{40}{7}$ 28. $\frac{15}{10}$ 29. $\frac{14}{12}$ 30. $\frac{42}{11}$
31. $\frac{16}{9}$ 32. $\frac{12}{7}$

### Lesson 6.1, Page 102
1. $\frac{6}{8}$ 2. $\frac{4}{16}$ 3. $\frac{10}{15}$ 4. $\frac{2}{4}$ 5. $\frac{6}{18}$ 6. $\frac{12}{48}$ 7. $\frac{10}{14}$ 8. $\frac{12}{24}$ 9. $\frac{8}{32}$
10. $\frac{6}{36}$ 11. $\frac{9}{27}$ 12. $\frac{12}{18}$ 13. $\frac{3}{15}$ 14. $\frac{2}{20}$ 15. $\frac{9}{12}$ 16. $\frac{9}{18}$ 17. $\frac{4}{12}$
18. $\frac{8}{16}$ 19. $\frac{2}{24}$ 20. $\frac{6}{18}$

### Lesson 6.2, Page 103
1. < 2. = 3. > 4. > 5. < 6. < 7. = 8. > 9. >

### Lesson 6.3, Page 104
1. > 2. = 3. < 4. < 5. = 6. =

### Lesson 6.4, Page 105
1. $\frac{11}{12}$ 2. $\frac{3}{5}$ 3. $\frac{5}{6}$ 4. $\frac{4}{10}$ 5. $\frac{5}{8}$ 6. $\frac{2}{3}$ 7. $\frac{3}{4}$ 8. $\frac{4}{5}$ 9. $\frac{9}{10}$
10. $\frac{5}{8}$ 11. $\frac{7}{12}$ 12. $\frac{2}{6}$ 13. $\frac{9}{10}$ 14. $\frac{8}{11}$ 15. $\frac{7}{7}$ or 1 16. $\frac{7}{9}$ 17. $\frac{11}{9}$

### Lesson 6.5, Page 106
1. $\frac{8}{12}$ 2. $\frac{4}{10}$ 3. $\frac{2}{4}$ 4. $\frac{1}{7}$ 5. $\frac{2}{10}$ 6. $\frac{1}{12}$ 7. $\frac{2}{5}$ 8. $\frac{3}{10}$ 9. $\frac{4}{8}$
10. $\frac{6}{10}$ 11. $\frac{7}{9}$ 12. $\frac{3}{11}$

### Lesson 6.6, Page 107
**1–4.** Answers will vary but should show two different ways to decompose each fraction using models and addition equations.

### Lesson 6.7, Page 108
1. $\frac{2}{3}$ 2. $\frac{1}{4}$ 3. $\frac{4}{5}$ 4. $\frac{6}{8}$

### Lesson 6.8, Page 109
1. 0.3 or $\frac{3}{10}$ 2. 0.7 or $\frac{7}{10}$ 3. 0.2 or $\frac{2}{10}$ 4. 0.2 5. 0.6
6. 0.9 7. 0.4 8. 0.3 9. 0.1 10. 0.8 11. 0.5
12–14.

### Lesson 6.9, Page 110
1. 0.30 or $\frac{30}{100}$ 2. 0.64 or $\frac{64}{100}$ 3. 0.98 or $\frac{98}{100}$ 4. 0.52 or $\frac{52}{100}$
5–7.

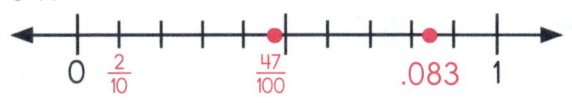

### Lesson 6.10, Page 111
1. $\frac{19}{100}$ 2. $\frac{22}{100}$ 3. $\frac{45}{100}$ 4. $\frac{77}{100}$ 5. $\frac{48}{100}$ 6. $\frac{65}{100}$ 7. $\frac{52}{100}$ 8. $\frac{36}{100}$ 9. $\frac{83}{100}$

### Lesson 6.11, Page 112
1. 9 2. 15 3. $10\frac{1}{3}$ 4. $7\frac{1}{5}$ 5. $11\frac{10}{11}$ 6. $12\frac{1}{5}$ 7. $9\frac{1}{2}$
8. $5\frac{1}{7}$ 9. $15\frac{1}{2}$

### Lesson 6.12, Page 113
1. $2\frac{1}{2}$ 2. $4\frac{1}{7}$ 3. $6\frac{1}{4}$ 4. $2\frac{7}{8}$ 5. $3\frac{1}{3}$ 6. $2\frac{3}{5}$
7. $2\frac{1}{5}$ 8. 2 9. $1\frac{5}{9}$

### Lesson 6.13, Page 114
1. 4 2. $8\frac{1}{2}$ 3. $4\frac{3}{5}$ 4. $2\frac{1}{4}$

### Lesson 6.14, Page 115
1. $7 \times \frac{1}{3}$ or $\frac{1}{3} + \frac{1}{3} + \frac{1}{3} + \frac{1}{3} + \frac{1}{3} + \frac{1}{3} + \frac{1}{3}$
2. $2 \times \frac{1}{8}$ or $\frac{1}{8} + \frac{1}{8}$ 3. $6 \times \frac{1}{10}$ or $\frac{1}{10} + \frac{1}{10} + \frac{1}{10} + \frac{1}{10} + \frac{1}{10} + \frac{1}{10}$ 4. $2 \times \frac{1}{4}$ or $\frac{1}{4} + \frac{1}{4}$ 5. $10 \times \frac{1}{6}$ or $\frac{1}{6} + \frac{1}{6} + \frac{1}{6} + \frac{1}{6} + \frac{1}{6} + \frac{1}{6} + \frac{1}{6} + \frac{1}{6} + \frac{1}{6} + \frac{1}{6}$ 6. $5 \times \frac{1}{12}$ or $\frac{1}{12} + \frac{1}{12} + \frac{1}{12} + \frac{1}{12} + \frac{1}{12}$

### Lesson 6.15, Page 116
1. $\frac{3}{8}$ 2. $3\frac{1}{3}$ 3. $1\frac{7}{9}$ 4. $1\frac{1}{7}$ 5. $3\frac{3}{5}$ 6. $1\frac{1}{9}$ 7. $\frac{6}{7}$ 8. $5\frac{1}{4}$
9. $3\frac{5}{9}$ 10. 4 11. $4\frac{4}{5}$ 12. 3

Spectrum Math Grade 4

# Answer Key

## Lesson 6.16, Page 117
1. $1\frac{1}{3}$  2. $1\frac{1}{7}$  3. $2\frac{1}{4}$  4. $6\frac{1}{4}$

## Posttest, Pages 118–119
1. 15  2. 6  3. 18  4. 40  5. >  6. <  7. >  8. >  9. $\frac{1}{2}$
10. $\frac{7}{9}$  11. $\frac{2}{3}$  12. $\frac{1}{5}$  13. $3 \times \frac{1}{5}$ or $\frac{1}{5} + \frac{1}{5} + \frac{1}{5}$
14. $\frac{1}{8} \times 7$ or $\frac{1}{8} + \frac{1}{8} + \frac{1}{8} + \frac{1}{8} + \frac{1}{8} + \frac{1}{8} + \frac{1}{8}$
15. $\frac{1}{6} \times 2$ or $\frac{1}{6} + \frac{1}{6}$  16. $\frac{1}{7} \times 5$ or $\frac{1}{7} + \frac{1}{7} + \frac{1}{7} + \frac{1}{7} + \frac{1}{7}$  17. 0.08  18. 0.4  19. 0.45  20. $\frac{13}{20}$  21. $3\frac{6}{7}$
22. $7\frac{7}{11}$  23. $\frac{33}{100}$  24. $3\frac{1}{3}$  25. $1\frac{2}{5}$  26. $3\frac{1}{9}$  27. 9
28. $7\frac{1}{9}$  29. $2\frac{1}{2}$  30. $1\frac{1}{8}$  31. $2\frac{6}{11}$  32. $\frac{3}{4}$  33. $4\frac{1}{2}$
34. $1\frac{1}{5}$  35. $2\frac{4}{5}$  36. $5\frac{1}{3}$

## Chapter 7
### Pretest, Pages 122–125
1. 1  2. 2  3. 8  4. 1,760  5. 24  6. 5  7. 1  8. 4  9. 20  10. 80; 300  11. 36; 72  12. 42°  13. 125°  14. 78°  15. 12  16. 6
17. 1,000  18. 25  19. 5,000  20. 60  21. 600  22. 32,000
23. 720  24. 19,000  25. 1,000  26. 1  27. 25,000  28. 20
29. 17,000  30. 52  31. $1\frac{3}{4}$ miles  32. $44\frac{1}{2}$ miles  33. 72
34. 17  35. 9  36. 20,000  37. 4,000  38. 50  39. 39,000

### Lesson 7.1, Page 126
1. 15  2. 96  3. 216  4. 4  5. 5,280  6. 864  7. 1,000  8. 2
9. 10,560  10. 1  11. 936  12. 4  13. 10  14. 120  15. 2,160
16. 12,320  17. 200  18. 108

### Lesson 7.2, Page 127
1. 36  2. 5  3. 21  4. 9

### Lesson 7.3, Page 128
1. 8  2. 2  3. 6  4. 6  5. 2  6. 20  7. 7  8. 7  9. 28  10. 24
11. 4  12. 7  13. 40  14. 60  15. 9  16. 48  17. 11  18. 8

### Lesson 7.4, Page 129
1. 2  2. 3  3. 8,000  4. 640  5. 4  6. 12  7. 0.5  8. 0.5  9. 9
10. 128  11. 192  12. 5  13. 10,000  14. 2  15. 96,000  16. 1

### Lesson 7.5, Page 130
1. 100  2. 30,000  3. 30,064  4. 48

### Lesson 7.6, Page 131
1. 400  2. 25,000  3. 21,000  4. 250  5. 3,330  6. 14,000
7. 1,500  8. 47,000  9. 5,000  10. 840  11. 7,500  12. 200
13. 10,000  14. 66,000  15. 210

### Lesson 7.7, Page 132
1. 3,000  2. 12,000  3. 2,000  4. 75,000  5. 10,000
6. 50,000  7. 13,000  8. 78,000  9. 8,000  10. 9  11. 7
12. 2

### Lesson 7.8, Page 133
1. 16,000  2. 32,000  3. 45,000  4. 10,000  5. 42,000
6. 9,000  7. 105,000  8. 37,000  9. 12,000  10. 183,000
11. 18,000  12. 119,000  13. 9  14. 45,000  15. 6

### Lesson 7.9, Page 134
1. 500  2. 5  3. 16  4. 10

### Lesson 7.10, Page 135
1. 14  2. 30  3. 28  4. 225  5. 120  6. 52

### Lesson 7.11, Page 136
1. 195  2. 121  3. 132  4. 250  5. 40  6. 480

### Lesson 7.12, Page 137
1. 100  2. 600  3. 4,125  4. 52

### Lesson 7.13, Page 138
1. 78 cups  2. 4 recipes  3. 2 cups

### Lesson 7.14, Page 139
1. right  2. acute  3. obtuse  4. acute  5. right
6. obtuse

### Lesson 7.15, Page 140
1. 60  2. 90  3. 110  4. 170  5. 90  6. 30  7–8. Check students' work.

# Answer Key

### Lesson 7.16, Page 141
1. 45  2. 75  3. 68  4. 75  5. 78  6. 28  7. 47  8. 145

### Posttest, Pages 142–145
1. 48  2. 80  3. 4,000  4. 1  5. 9  6. 45  7. 3  8. 14
9. 5  10. 44  11. 45  12. 390  13. 225  14. 137,000
15. 200  16. 8  17. 336  18. 60  19. 2.5  20. 13,000
21. 400  22. 37,000  23. 15,000  24. 44,000
25. 9,000  26. 950  27. 2,200  28. 4  29. $\frac{6}{8}$  30. 7
31. 48  32. 96  33–35. Check students' work.  36. 70
37. 45  38. 50  39. 20

## Chapter 8
### Pretest, Page 148
1. MNL or LNM  2. QRS or SRQ  3–5. Drawings will vary.  6–9. AWV but should include at least one line of symmetry.  10. rectangle
11. isosceles and right

### Lesson 8.1, Page 149
1. $\overrightarrow{QP}$ and $\overrightarrow{QR}$, Q, ∠PQR and ∠RQP  2. $\overrightarrow{ED}$ or $\overrightarrow{EF}$, E, ∠DEF or ∠FED  3–4. AWV  5–6. Drawings will vary.

### Lesson 8.2, Page 150
1. intersecting  2. parallel  3. perpendicular
E: AWV

### Lesson 8.2, Page 151
1–3. Drawings will vary but should match the type noted.  4. parallel lines: $\overleftrightarrow{AB}$ and $\overleftrightarrow{CD}$, $\overleftrightarrow{AC}$ and $\overleftrightarrow{BD}$; perpendicular lines: $\overleftrightarrow{AC}$ and $\overleftrightarrow{AB}$, $\overleftrightarrow{CD}$ and $\overleftrightarrow{BD}$, $\overleftrightarrow{AC}$ and $\overleftrightarrow{CD}$, $\overleftrightarrow{AB}$ and $\overleftrightarrow{BD}$  5. parallel lines: $\overleftrightarrow{EF}$ and $\overleftrightarrow{HG}$, $\overleftrightarrow{EH}$ and $\overleftrightarrow{FG}$  6. perpendicular lines: $\overleftrightarrow{XY}$ and $\overleftrightarrow{YZ}$

### Lesson 8.3, Page 152
1. yes  2. yes  3. yes  4. yes  5. no  6. no

### Lesson 8.3, Page 153
1–6. All are symmetrical. AWV but should show a line of symmetry.  E: A square has four lines of symmetry. A circle has infinite lines of symmetry.

### Lesson 8.4, Page 154
1. rectangle  2. trapezoid  3. parallelogram
4. trapezoid  5. parallelogram  6. rhombus

### Lesson 8.5, Page 155
1. isosceles and right  2. scalene  3. isosceles and obtuse  4. equilateral  E: Because you are combining angles and side lengths.

### Posttest, Pages 156–157
1–4. AWV but should show a correct line of symmetry.  5. parallel  6. perpendicular
7. perpendicular  8. parallel  9–11. Check students' work.  12. trapezoid  13. scalene and right

## Chapter 9
### Pretest, Pages 160–161
1. +5  2. −100  3. ×2  4. ÷10  5. +2, +3, +4, +5
6. +6  7. 10, 12, 14  8. 40, 30, 20  9. 80, 160, 320
10. 55, 66, 77  11. 81  12. 43  13. 21

### Lesson 9.1, Page 162
1. 29, 35, +6  2. 39, 48, +9  3. 88, 90, +2  4. 587, 592, +5  5. 144, 149, +5  6. 100, 103, +3  7.

### Lesson 9.2, Page 163
1. 51, 41, −10  2. 12, 7, −5  3. 24, 18, −6  4. 400, 395, −5
5. 155, 147, −8  6. 600, 575, −25  7.

### Lesson 9.3, Page 164
1. 16, 32, ×2  2. 81, 243, ×3  3. 625, 3,125, ×5
4. 10,000, 100,000, ×10  5. 1,296, 7,776, ×6
E: AWV

Spectrum Math Grade 4

191

# Answer Key

### Lesson 9.4, Page 165
1. 2, ÷5  2. 1, ÷10  3. 3, ÷3  4. 4, ÷4  E: AWV

### Lesson 9.5, Page 166
1. 14, 18, 24, 32  2. 84, 82, 79, 75  3. 6, 8, 11, 15
4. 69, 63, 54, 42  5. 23 should be circled, +5, +6, +7, . . .  6. 60 should be circled, −10, −9, −8, . . .

### Lesson 9.6, Page 167
1. 60  2. 5, 20, 80, 320, 1,280, 5,120, 20,480  3. 192
4. 25

### Posttest, Pages 168–169
1. +2, +3, +4, . . .  2. +1, +2, +3, . . .  3. ÷2  4. −9
5. 13, 15  6. 4, 2  7. 36, 9  8. 360, 250  9. 203, 207, 211, 215  10. 11, 22, 44, 88  11. 24  12. 24  13. 31

### Learning Checkpoint, Pages 170–174
1. $\frac{16}{32}$  2. $\frac{5}{15}$  3. =  4. >  5. $\frac{10}{12}$ or $\frac{5}{6}$  6. $1\frac{2}{8}$ or $1\frac{1}{4}$  7. $\frac{1}{5}$
8. $\frac{4}{12}$ or $\frac{1}{3}$  9. $3 \times \frac{1}{9}$ or $\frac{1}{9} + \frac{1}{9} + \frac{1}{9}$  10. 0.8 or $\frac{8}{10}$
11. 0.5 or $\frac{5}{10}$  12. 0.71 or $\frac{71}{100}$  13. $16\frac{4}{5}$  14. $10\frac{1}{3}$  15. $3\frac{3}{7}$
16. $\frac{12}{25}$  17. $3\frac{1}{3}$  18. $\frac{11}{50}$  19. $12\frac{1}{5}$  20. $13\frac{3}{4}$  21. $2\frac{1}{3}$  22. $\frac{1}{5}$
23. $1\frac{5}{7}$  24. $\frac{6}{7}$  25. 1  26. 2  27. 8  28. 1,760  29. 24
30. 5  31. 80, 300  32. 36, 72  33. 43°  34. 124°  35. 80°
36. 16  37. 6  38. 1,000  39. 1  40. 17,000  41. 72  42. 17
43. 9  44. ∠LNM or ∠MNL  45. ∠PQR or ∠RQP
46–47. Drawings will vary.  48–49. Check students' work.  50. rectangle  51. isoceles  52. 50, 25; −25
53. 11, 13, 15; +2  54. 498, 494; −4  55. 9, 3; ÷3

### Final Test, Pages 175–182
1. 36  2. 1,964  3. 790  4. 285  5. 980  6. 1,054
7. 4,330  8. 12,750  9. 1,055  10. 3,659  11. 31,168
12. 11,122  13. 27,760  14. 21,688  15. 67,123
16. 376,484  17. 91  18. 79  19. 48  20. 39  21. 53
22. 527  23. 5,269  24. 1,532  25. 2,136  26. 455
27. 429  28. 1,281  29. 702  30. 873  31. 448
32. 384  33. 9,604  34. 1,170  35. 1,728  36. 4,158
37. 4,212  38. 3,112  39. 1,720  40. 494  41. 14,070
42. 4,006  43. 31,776  44. 23,724  45. 15  46. 8
47. 10  48. 18 r4  49. 82 r1  50. 291  51. 125  52. 197 r2
53. 371 r1  54. 2,641  55. 938 r3  56. 2,409 r1  57. 1,638 r4  58. 625  59. 1,400 r4  60. 730 r1
61. 2,000 + 200 + 30 + 7  62. 300 + 90 + 7
63. 50,000 + 5,000 + 600 + 8  64. 60,000 + 9,000 + 700 + 30 + 5  65. 103,500  66. 1,800,000
67. 23,000  68. 580  69. >  70. <  71. >  72. 1  73. $\frac{1}{3}$
74. $1\frac{1}{4}$  75. 1  76. 4  77. 20  78. <  79. <  80. >  81. 0.8
82. 0.07  83. 0.3  84. 0.65  85. 1  86. 70  87. 10,000
88. 14,000  89. 72,000  90. 44  91. 11  92. 40  93. 44
94. 150  95. 176  96. 300  97. 90°  98. 47°  99. 128°
100–102. Drawings will vary.  103. intersecting
104. perpendicular  105. parallel  106. 54, 57
107. 55, 44  108. 1,010, 1,000  109. 225, 275
110–113. Check students' work.  114. 8  115. $2\frac{1}{5}$
116. $2\frac{1}{2}$  117. $8\frac{2}{7}$  118. $7\frac{1}{9}$  119. $1\frac{1}{6}$  120. $5\frac{1}{4}$  121. $1\frac{1}{7}$

192

Spectrum Math Grade 4